CHASING

THE

WHITE

RABBIT

CHASING

THE

WHITE

RABBIT

A DISCOVERY OF LEADERSHIP IN THE 21ST CENTURY

Lessons from the
Battlefield to the Boardroom

DANIEL & DAVID MORGAN

Published by Advantage, Charleston, South Carolina.
Member of Advantage Media Group.

ADVANTAGE is a registered trademark and the Advantage colophon is a trademark of Advantage Media Group, Inc.

Printed in the United States of America.

ISBN: 978-1-59932-647-4
LCCN: 2015959231

This publication is designed to provide accurate and authoritative information in regard to the subject matter covered. It is sold with the understanding that the publisher is not engaged in rendering legal, accounting, or other professional services. If legal advice or other expert assistance is required, the services of a competent professional person should be sought.

Advantage Media Group is proud to be a part of the Tree Neutral® program. Tree Neutral offsets the number of trees consumed in the production and printing of this book by taking proactive steps such as planting trees in direct proportion to the number of trees used to print books. To learn more about Tree Neutral, please visit www.treeneutral.com. To learn more about Advantage's commitment to being a responsible steward of the environment, please visit www.advantagefamily.com/green

Advantage Media Group is a publisher of business, self-improvement, and professional development books and online learning. We help entrepreneurs, business leaders, and professionals share their Stories, Passion, and Knowledge to help others Learn & Grow. Do you have a manuscript or book idea that you would like us to consider for publishing? Please visit advantagefamily.com or call 1.866.775.1696.

To my wife, Patty, and children, Isabel and Gabriel, who have stood by me during tough times. Their love and resiliency for our family and those families who have given the ultimate sacrifice can never be expressed in words. And to my parents, brothers, and sister, who have always had confidence in me, even when I stood on the brink of wrong choices.

—Dan Morgan

For my wife, Amy, my family, and all of the people I have had the pleasure of working with and for. Their collective support gave me the courage to continue the struggle to be a better person, husband, brother, and son.

—David Morgan

From both of us, we could not be who we are today without the sacrifice and service of those we have served: soldiers, firefighters, and staffs.

ACKNOWLEDGMENTS

This book could not have been written without the patience, leadership, and mentorship of people I have served within various capacities.

Foremost, I cannot express enough my admiration for our nation's soldiers. Their values of honor, personal courage, and integrity are unmatched. Leadership is a lifestyle choice, and leading these warfighters has been a blessing. I stand where I stand now because I stand on their shoulders. I also cannot forget how important my soldier peers are to my life. I learn from them every day and appreciate their support and advice to my family and me. My heartfelt gratitude goes to Jason Norton, Brett Funck, Herve Clermont, Steve Michael, Derek Jansen, Bob Culp, Mike Oeschger, Keith McKinley, Michael Larsen, Bill Ryan, Jason Gentile, Matthew Hardman, David Bass, Jeff Farmer, Jeremy Peifer, and others too long to list. And I cannot forego the opportunity to thank all of their spouses for their support to our Soldiers and to my beautiful wife and children.

I also want to thank General Barry McCaffrey for his mentorship and presence in my life from our times in the Clinton White House and through the last fifteen years of war. His candor and drive in standards and discipline in how to win on the battlefield and in any mission at hand is second to none. My time under his tutelage changed my life. If it were not for his leadership, I would not have gained the focus I needed to support him in the execution of

President Bill Clinton's National Drug Control Strategy and then to lead our cherished men and women in uniform during the crucible of ground combat.

Last, I want to thank Generals David Petraeus, Mark Milley, John Campbell, and Mike Scaparrotti; Lieutenant Generals Steve Townsend, Joe Anderson, Jim McConville, and Steve Lanza; and finally, Brigadier John "Pete" Johnson. These senior military officers have provided a positive environment while preparing for combat and in the most difficult of situations. Their presence, grit, and caring can only be repaid by every ounce of effort I can give to our men and women in uniform. Their trust and stewardship in me showed me how leadership can enable people to accomplish more than I ever thought possible.

—Dan Morgan

Throughout my life, there have been countless people that have impacted my views on what true leadership represents. From my early volunteer experiences beginning in high school at a food bank feeding the homeless to being able to participate in discussions with industry and public service leaders of all levels, the true meaning of leadership evolves with every new experience. At times, leadership can be exhilarating and other times exhausting. It comes from a deep understanding of yourself and belief in something greater that drives you to make a positive impact in others' lives.

From my times in public service as a volunteer firefighter and paramedic, there were countless everyday leaders who worked their "day jobs" and then came home and dedicated their lives to helping people that they did not know. Many of them sacrificed time away from their families at great peril to themselves, not for glory or fame but for each other and a belief that they could make a difference. Unfortunately, I cannot acknowledge them all, but I want to specifically pay recognition to Rich Takacs, Eric Globerman, Richard Sien, Mark and Michelle Arsenuault, Chuck Fusco, and Ron Blackwell. I am honored to have worked with these individuals; they allowed me to learn "on the job" what it takes to lead an organization, and they had the patience to forgive and forget all the mistakes I made. Without them and all the other members of the organizations that I worked with, I would never have had the passion and courage to stand in the shadow of those that went before me and lead an organization with such a storied past and such a promising future.

During my professional life, I have had the privilege to be able to meet and work with accomplished leaders from industry, military, and government. Whether walking the halls of Congress or working in the Pentagon or meeting with heads of industry-leading companies, I learned that, above all, leadership is firmly rooted in a strong foundation of ethics and sense of purpose that transcends self. While I have had the honor of meeting a number of great people that have shaped my view on business leadership, I must acknowledge the following people that have made a life-lasting impression on me: Andrew Sherman, for his rabbi-like wisdom and honesty; Russ Ackoff, for shaping my ideas on idealized design and how it relates to leadership; and Barry McCaffrey, for all the hours of counsel and advice on leadership and vision.

Finally, I must acknowledge my father, Ted, and my younger brother, Doug. We have had our challenges and successes in business, but if it were not for their support, hard work, and commitment, we would not have the success we enjoy today.

Only those who have stepped out on the field of competition with everything at stake and lost a battle—but still show up to fight another day, a bit wiser and humbler—understand what courage it really takes to lead.

—David Morgan

FOREWORD

The first requirements of a great leader are more likely to be character and determination rather than extreme intelligence. Sure it helps enormously to not be stupid; wisdom and clarity of thinking allow you to worry about the right things. However, the first thing you must look for in an up-and-coming leader is character. What we need today are steadfast leaders of high character that can develop and maximize teams to accomplish things greater than they believed possible. In their first book, *Chasing the White Rabbit*, Dan and Dave Morgan demonstrate these qualities through their lessons.

After a long career in the military, public service, and private industry, I have been fortunate to serve with many, many exemplary leaders. General Colin Powell, Secretary of Defense Bill Perry, General Gordon Sullivan, Dr. Barry Karlin of CRC, Steve Barnes in Bain Capital, Ramsey Musallum in Veritas Capital, and many others are examples of successful leadership while serving in very difficult, challenging situations. These leaders learned to surround themselves with great people who will challenge their ideas and assumptions, while empowering and developing them.

I have known Colonel Dan Morgan professionally for almost twenty years. He worked for me when I was President Bill Clinton's Director of the White House Office of National Drug Control Policy. He personally accompanied me as my lead troubleshooter on dozens of missions around the globe and in the United States. His leadership and ability to see through the fog of politics helped me to successfully deal with the administration, the US Congress, and with leaders of many nations around the world. Since 2001, Dan has been continuously involved in combat, serving with enormous courage in both Iraq and Afghanistan. Senior military leaders have consistently relied on his leadership in critical combat positions. He commanded elite units at company and battalion level in combat and also served at high-level operational staffs in both conflicts.

I met Dave Morgan in 2001 upon my departure from public service and served on his firm's advisory board. Since 2001, I worked alongside Dave as an advisor in a number of strategic opportunities and viewed his personal and professional growth. Dave has led his company into one of the fastest-growing small businesses in America. Dave has always shown a unique ability to communicate and motivate his team and establish meaningful relationships with his partners and peers around industry. His calm demeanor in the face of stressful situations is clearly apparent from over twenty years of volunteer service in the midst of chaos at emergencies and ultimately leading as a fire chief.

In developing this book, you can see how Dan and Dave Morgan go beyond bureaucratic leadership and focus on earning trust and respect with people in their organizations. Although the experiences of the two of them are very different, these two superb men prove that the fundamentals of leadership transcend across careers. They demonstrate that personal convictions, principles, and constant personal growth allow leaders to develop and flourish. The two Morgan brothers recognize that technology can create a dangerous illusion that many leaders may only think they know what is going on in their organization. Dan and Dave are not leaders of presence—they are engaged leaders. These two brothers have provided great insights into self-awareness and how to build skills and character for the 21st century. This book is a hugely useful and interesting personal primer on leadership development.

—General Barry R. McCaffrey, former President Bill Clinton's Director of the White House Office of National Drug Control Policy and former Commanding General, US Southern Command

TABLE OF CONTENTS

PART 3
HOW DO WE DO IT?
-113-

PART 4
WHO DO YOU SEE IN THE MIRROR?
-157-

INTRODUCTION

We are brothers who, like many people, were unfocused on a purpose in our younger years and sometimes took the wrong paths in finding our way in life. Back then, admittedly, our bad habits outweighed our good ones. In spite of our inauspicious early years, we managed over time to achieve considerable success in our fields—one in the military, the other in private business and the public safety realm. And over time, we learned through self-discovery that the journey is what made us leaders.

Over the years, we compared stories of our experiences and realized that even though we took different paths in life, those paths converged in one key area—leadership. We discovered that leadership was not only a journey but also a quest. It wove itself into our lives, leading to a self-discovery from who we were to who we are now and finally to whom we want to be. Leadership, we learned, does not just happen—it demands a conscious lifestyle choice. Why is it a lifestyle choice? Because leadership means being responsible for the welfare of people and organizations, and that requires character, competence, and commitment.

We grew up and worked together while in college, but after college our lives diverged, and we had completely different experiences in our adult life. But in both of our professions, we started seeing a new dynamic in today's environment, where more and more people struggle to understand their purpose in an organization: who they are, what they want to be, what they're supposed to do, and how they're supposed to achieve it.

We wanted to write this book to share some personal experiences as a way of demonstrating the critical nature of leadership. That nature is the pursuit of purpose, or meaning, for you as a leader, for the people around you, and for your organization. You must serve and give to others, not take. This selflessness and stewardship for others and something bigger than you is leadership, for it gives you meaning in your life and others' lives.

Rather than give you a step-by-step "how to" or recipe of what you can do to be a leader, we decided to paint a picture for you of what a leader looks like by sharing our experiences. Why? Because neither of us subscribes to the idea that reading a list of thought processes or personality traits will automatically turn you into a leader. It won't. Leadership is a continually evolving process: physically, intellectually, and emotionally. It is an action-and-results-driven journey that is reinforced through lifelong learning and feedback.

Make no mistake: We don't discount reading and studying—leaders must constantly seek to learn and obtain feedback. They are gifts. Unfortunately, many leadership books cite certain personality traits and other characteristics that a person must possess in order to lead. This may help, but it is not an end-all solution. All great leaders study and adapt, but first, if you desire to lead others, you must align your own character values to the values of an organization for genuine leader development. This can take time, either within an organization or across different organizations, but commitment is what reigns supreme. This journey will drive your pursuit of purpose to lead others in a values-based organization so that you can serve those around you—for something bigger than yourself.

In this book, we share our personal discoveries about leadership and how we got to where we are today. Most of the book contains our observations about leadership—our own experiences and some that we've witnessed. In each chapter, we also include a story or two about our experiences as they pertain to the topic of the chapter: These stories may be about a success or a failure, and some are about loss of life. We have carefully chosen these stories because we believe each one will challenge you to think about what we may have done wrong or right.

We hope that our experiences and observations will spark some self-discoveries that you can take on your own leadership journey to help guide you through challenging times. Remember, this journey is a lifestyle choice, full of overwhelming emotions ranging from pride to utter despair; just when you think you understand the environment, it will change. These experiences can be exceptionally rewarding but can also challenge your will and commitment to lead others responsibly and with integrity.

That's what makes *Alice in Wonderland* the perfect analogy. In *Alice in Wonderland*, Alice's story is set in motion as she follows her curiosity and chases a white rabbit down a rabbit hole, touching off a series of adventures in an unfamiliar land. Alice's experience is a lot like leadership: once you go down the rabbit hole of assuming a leadership role, you'll discover that the world looks much different than the one you're comfortable with. Throughout these pages, we use the idea of Alice's white rabbit to signify challenges and opportunities leaders face in today's environment. The rabbit and his holes cannot be limited to a specific definition, and they cannot always be predicted. In today's world of multigenerational leaders, fast pace of change and information, and drive for innovation, jumping into a new environment and finding oneself in a place of unhinged experiences has become the norm rather than the exception. In this book, we describe our journey into various rabbit holes. Our experiences will hopefully enlighten other leaders in deciding whether or not to chase a certain white rabbit down a hole, and, if you do, how to best manage the experience.

Today, these experiences are driven by fast-changing technology and increased velocity of instability and conflict in the world, which is like nothing we've seen before. Rapid innovation in technology, global economic competition over resources, and ideological conflicts in places like the Middle East are changing everything. Global and regional security, traditional alliances and partnerships, business and economic practices, and globalized personal interaction are all inter-secting at such a pace that many of the old paradigms no longer apply. Leaders must embrace the change by becoming inventive, innovative, and creative spirits in their organization

In chasing the white rabbit and jumping down these "holes," if you will, or walking through various "doorways" of life, we've typically seen that leaders are challenged in how to understand or manage some of the complexities that are going on in this environ-ment. What we have learned is that one constant binds unhinged experiences—people. Despite all these changes, people provide the glue to drive an organization's values, purpose, and goals. Everything else only enables people, and leadership is what aligns values, goals, and people. If you keep this in mind, then leaders will possess the confidence to jump into any rabbit hole in order to lead an organiza-tion on a path to success.

So we hope our sometimes simple, sometimes complex stories can draw out some thoughts on how you can venture on your own journey and be better than both of us. That is our goal—to help future leaders develop a sense of purpose in being part of something bigger than themselves.

Who Is Dan Morgan?

Over the years, I've felt myself going through experiences—much like Alice in Wonderland—except the new worlds that I entered landed me in increasing levels of responsibility. My journey chasing the rabbit down rabbit holes defined life and leadership for me as taking the responsibility to find solutions for problems and fulfill the goals or tasks, which life constantly sets for people and their organization.

In high school, I wasn't focused on preparing for the next phase of life; I was an athlete, but I spent a lot of time going out, drinking beer, and just generally drifting without fully understanding how important it was to prepare myself for college.

Instead of going straight to college after graduation from high school, I enlisted in the military, where I learned the importance of responsibility—for myself, to others, and to a common mission or goal. These are values I had never really understood in my younger years, even though I played team sports while in school. When I came home to go to college, I began to see how these values equated to success in life.

In spite of my lack of focus in high school, after my service in the military I went to a community college and the University of Maryland for a year, and then I transferred to Georgetown University in Washington, D.C. This achievement was my first step in my leadership journey. I took responsibility for myself. After graduation from Georgetown (with a grade point average that was a far cry from my 1.77 high school GPA), I returned to the military as a US Army Infantry officer.

In the military, I attended multiple schools, including Airborne, Ranger, Jumpmaster, and other great leadership and training schools. I was assigned to an Airborne Combat Team in Vicenza, Italy, in the early 1990s, where we participated in and supported multiple deployments in the Balkans and Africa. During a parachute jump at the end of my tour, I blew out my right knee and returned to D.C. to undergo surgery and a year of rehabilitation. During this period, I was fortunate enough to be accepted to Georgetown University's prestigious School of Foreign Service, where I earned my master's degree in National Security Strategic Studies. My responsibilities grew even more during my recovery, when I met and married my wife. Those responsibilities would increase a few years later when we had our first child. My sense of purpose, or meaning, was beginning to crystallize.

After my year of rehabilitation, I was fortunate to land the role of executive assistant to General Barry R. McCaffrey, who was the nation's drug czar for the White House Office of National Drug Control Policy. General McCaffrey is a national treasure—a warrior, a diplomat, and an exemplary father and husband. In that role, I traveled all around the world and was introduced to people from every walk of life, from prisoners and pregnant women who were addicted to drugs to heads of state of foreign countries like China, Colombia, and others. Through these experiences with different cultures, I saw that young people and the leaders of young people were struggling with some of the same problems that we struggle with here in America, particularly with regard to the impact of drugs and alcohol, poverty, education, and other social ailments. But the common thread woven through everyone was leadership through values, purpose, and goals.

I began to see a shared consciousness among senior government and military leaders to reinforce organizational values and ethics; it was an effort by leaders to do what they believed was the right thing for people, whether it was for their own nation, for a particular organization, or for just a shared set of tasks and purpose. The experience was a crucible for me, enhanced by assisting General McCaffrey in the West Wing with President Bill Clinton or in the White House Situation Room or during Congress or Senate testimonies where I helped develop policy to aid people—here in our nation or among our allies and partners across the globe.

That's when I discovered that I needed to align myself with a values-based, service-oriented, and purposeful organization. To me, that meant leaving the political arena and returning to active duty in the military. When the Clinton administration ended, General McCaffrey also left office. We left the White House after his farewell, shook hands on the corner of 17th and Pennsylvania in front of the White House and Old Executive Building, and said good-bye. Four days later, I was back in uniform with the Screaming Eagle patch and assigned to the 101st Airborne Division.

Some seven months later, the attack on the World Trade Center took place.

Since then, I have been constantly training and equipping soldiers, and I have deployed to Iraq and Afghanistan five times for yearlong deployments. In short, for eleven years I was either in a combat zone or preparing to go back to a combat zone.

Through it all, I have seen a large number of fallen and wounded heroes, and it has been quite a struggle to ensure our soldiers continue to believe in me as their commander, believe in the leaders that they report directly to, and believe in each other. Most of the time, this is not that difficult a task, but during times of extended combat deployment, when soldiers have constant access to information from political pundits and media over the Internet, I have had to make sure that they continue to believe in the mission as well. And I have been amazed that our service members—even if they don't necessarily fully believe in the mission—understand the values of the organization that they're a part of, believe in each other to the point of fighting and dying for each other, and maintain their oath to the Constitution of the United States.

After serving in combat in Iraq and Afghanistan—as company commander, battalion operations officer, brigade operations officer, and division chief of operations with the 101st Airborne Division's Screaming Eagles—I then became a battalion commander in 10th Mountain Division, followed by service as a chief of staff for the 10th Mountain Division's rear headquarters.

Today, I am a full colonel and in command of Joint Base Lewis-McChord, our nation's premier and only power projection platform for a joint force. I remain aligned with the values of my Army. I love being a part of something bigger than myself, hope to make positive change, and love serving those people around me. My life has meaning because I am part of something bigger than me.

Looking back, I realize that I've had good habits and bad habits, the latter of which I've had to change or manage in order for me to be relevant and succeed in my life as a mature adult. It takes physical and moral courage, teamwork, discipline, and willpower to learn and develop as a leader. It is doable. If you could only have seen where I was as an eighteen-year-old or single lieutenant in Italy!

Who Is David Morgan?

After I got out of high school, I planned to attend medical school, but in college I spent too much time working in bars and not enough time at study. Needless to say, I did not do my best when it came to grades, which ultimately were inadequate for me to get into medical school—even though I tested well on the medical college admission test and was wait-listed several times.

In trying to fulfill my dream of being in medicine, I decided to build up my credentials, and one of the more practical ways to do that was by volunteering with the county fire department; I started by becoming a firefighter/EMT and ultimately a paramedic in a unit that was heavily oriented toward emergency medical services and specialty rescue. I also worked in a private doctor's office—an allergy and asthma clinic—where I worked in the lab and assisted with patient care. I spent a lot of time at Georgetown Hospital, helped teach cardiac life-support classes in the medical school, and worked in the hospital's pediatric mobile clinic, which went into poorer parts of Washington, D.C. to treat underprivileged kids.

Ultimately, my pursuit of practical work experience and all the exposure as a healthcare provider led me to decide that medicine wasn't for me, although I would end up staying with the volunteer fire department for two decades.

About the time I was going to enter medical school, my father asked me if I wanted to start a company with him. Looking back, without realizing it at the time, this was a pivotal milestone in my journey. I had always seen myself in medicine, but the idea of entrepreneurship was too intriguing to pass up. Together we started STS International, an engineering and technical services solutions firm that offers systems engineering, communications development, and medical simulation software. Our primary client is the US Department of Defense.

When we started the company, we landed a couple of major projects. I became program manager over a project for the Department of the Army by default, but I really had no understanding of what it meant to be in such an influential role. Then one day, about six months into the position, I was standing in a room with the command leadership of the US Special Operation Command—some of the most powerful people in the US military—and we were conversing about how to address the next ten to fifteen years of the Department of Defense's approach to biometrics.

That's when I knew what I wanted to do; I went from being someone trying to decide what career to pursue to being a person who was leading and making decisions and struggling with how to resolve extremely complex problems.

Over the next three years, we grew the company from five to seventy-five employees, most of which were twenty years my senior. Today, STS has been in business for twenty-five years, and I'm heavily involved in speaking on entrepreneurship and leadership at the University of Maryland. On occasion I also have opportunities to speak at Georgetown Law.

I stayed with the volunteer fire department for over twenty years, and I continued to do that work alongside my job in the corporate realm. The volunteer public safety industry is a very tightly woven, community-oriented group of people, and I quickly progressed through the ranks into leadership positions. Ultimately, I became chief of our department, president, and a member of the board, roles I remained in for ten years.

I found being a leader in this organization to be a very eye-opening experience. In managing a membership of over two hundred volunteers and having to get them to do things that weren't necessarily based on pay and that often involved trauma and mourning, I learned a lot about how to motivate people. Empathy plays a big part in that because not everyone is of the same mind-set; some people are there to run into burning buildings, some want to help with administration, some just to be part of a community.

My volunteer experience also helped me a lot in business; it helped me to see that, at the end of the day, most employees just want to be managed and told that they're doing a good job and that there's a reason for what they're doing.

For the most part, there has been no road map in my life that has allowed me to progress and develop professionally. As in most leadership roles, the results of my actions were felt very personally and with little chance for safe harbor and feedback from peers. The reality was that a bad decision could result in very real impacts: a loss of someone's property or life in the fire department or going bankrupt and losing my house in business. It seemed that every day there was a new challenge that I was ill-prepared for, and at times I had no idea what to do. I had to create from what we knew and leap into a decision with a tremendous fear of the unknown.

So the last twenty years of my life have been a constant evolution of new opportunities and challenges—a constant pursuit of that white rabbit—where I have had to make a decision and people are looking to me for guidance, a place where I've had to continually rely on my values, purpose, and goals in making decisions. It's a place I feel very comfortable in.

What Is Leadership?

For us, leadership boils down to taking responsibility for people who have a shared set of values, purpose, and goals: that applies whether you're with your family, friends, or business associates; whether you're at home, in the community, in the boardroom, or on the battlefield; and whether you're in charge of the business, a worker trying to make a living, or a member of a military unit.

There is a salient point between both domains—military and commercial. No matter where you are, you're a leader to some degree; you are responsible for yourself and others and for the values, goals, and purpose of the organization you're a part of.

Consequently, you must be open and understand that there will be successes and failures and that you will learn from them. Being a leader is about understanding who you are and that you must accept responsibility for the decisions you make, whether they were exceptionally good or exceptionally bad. Leaders must also let people make their own decisions, as long as those decisions are not illegal or unethical and not detrimental to the values, purpose, and goals of the organization.

How does a leader take in everything happening around him and still arrive at a place where there's an understanding of values and a mission? And then how does he translate those values and that mission to the rest of the team?

Leadership is also about taking charge of your own life and creating your own framework for success, and then, once you've done that, how do you expand that to your family and professional career?

In the pages that follow, you'll find no-nonsense information that can be of help in current multigenerational leadership challenges, whether you are a college-level student or junior to senior leader in business or government service. Today's fast-paced environment seems to have become enamored with technology, driving ideas, concepts, capabilities, and decisions. This trend contributes to a belief that technology can lead to increased management and control in order to ensure better success. Unfortunately, this belief disregards what comes first—the human being. Leadership is about people first. Technology is only an enabler. Leaders serve people through values-based decision making—they don't serve technology and processes.

PART ONE

Who We Are

"In another moment, down went Alice after it, never once considering how in the world she was going to get out again."

L ike Alice of the famed *Alice in Wonderland* by Lewis Carroll, today's leaders often find themselves stepping over thresholds, or jumping through virtual doorways, into unfamiliar territory where the rules of the past no longer seem to apply. On this unfamiliar turf, where the players come from a multitude of dimensions, leaders are making decisions based on past experiences or learning, which often no longer seems valid amid a constantly changing landscape.

Through our personal experience and professional growth, our own experiences in "chasing white rabbits," we recognized our own change and that we are leaders of people older and younger, with less or more experience than we. On our journey, we've learned that the focus for leaders is the alignment of people with the values, goals, and purpose of an organization, not the alignment of technology for results.

Today, leadership is multigenerational, and senior leaders struggle to figure out how to deal with a world where change is outpacing anything experienced in the past. What was normal five years ago is not normal today. In the 21st century, yesterday's problem is today's solution, which only becomes tomorrow's problem. Take communication and information as examples of the dramatic changes our world has undergone: In our lifetimes, we've gone from rotary dial phones and hardbound encyclopedias to conversing via social media and relying on the Internet for instant information. Computers, the tools that make it so easy for our organizations to function in real time, can also bring work to a standstill when we become the victims of cyberhacking.

In this environment, it can be very difficult to understand where you fit as a leader, what and whom you are responsible for, and what do you do with that responsibility.

Navigating this landscape is crucial in today's environment, where there is a call to action for leaders to create a culture and climate of accountability for themselves and those they serve, while trying to develop their own confidence and ability to lead. People who want to lead or are thrust into leading must step back and reflect on their values, purpose, and goals.

This applies to leaders whether they are part of a military organization with hundreds of thousands of personnel following a defined direction, overseeing a volunteer organization of unpaid staff, or head of a family enterprise where members of a family determine the company's direction and profits.

In order to establish and nurture a purposeful organization, it's important for you, as a leader, to understand your values, purpose, and goals. You must know, as an individual, what you are trying to achieve and how that fits into an organization. This will help you frame your purpose and how you're going to interact with your organization and the people around you.

CHAPTER 1

Organizational Values, Purpose, and Goals

"How puzzling all these changes are! I'm never sure what I'm going to be, from one minute to another."

Alice's journey opened her eyes to a world of experiences that defined her during her journey. Chasing the white rabbit is about the discovery of uncertainty, the acceleration of change and information, and the desire to immediately act on or try and understand that information. But it is also about being comfortable with being uncomfortable. For leaders today, it is about who you are and how you fit in your organization during today's complex world.

This is a challenge for leaders of organizations today: How do you create and motivate a team in a world of unprecedented change caused by endless advances in technology and cultural integration on a global scale?

It takes a solid leader to move an organization forward in the environment we operate in today. Therefore, as an individual and a leader, you must:

- Identify your own values—this is key to your success as a leader. For example, a leader who prefers serving in a volunteer-like capacity will likely struggle to succeed in a profit-minded organization.

- Define your purpose in leading others. Values will underpin and help define this purpose, but again, those values must be congruent with the organization for success.

- Align your values with your purpose within an organization. This will enable you to develop goals. People can then commit to you and the organization.

- Enable leadership development and success through feedback. By aligning your values, purpose, and goals, you'll create an environment where others can grow and develop.

Throughout this book we'll continue to discuss the importance of values, purpose, and goals—both yours and the organization's—and we'll stress the relevance of your actions and deeds in aligning people with those key components.

Know Your Stakeholders

One of the first things you must do to lead people in today's fast-paced, multicultural, multinational environments is to understand who your decisions are impacting.

It's important to be able to pull information from different sectors of life—business, politics, or government. But in doing so, leaders often find themselves overwhelmed with all the opportunities or challenges presented to them by the commodity of free information.

That's why, as a leader, you must understand who your key stakeholders are and how your decisions impact them. Key stakeholders in any organization include yourself, your family, staff and employees, customers and suppliers, community members, and so on. Once you understand the framework of the people you're impacting and the degree of impact you have on them and they on your organization, then you can begin to determine whether the goals you set are achievable.

As you identify stakeholders, you must not overextend your organization's capacity or capabilities to meet stakeholders' interests. If you do, trust in you and your organization will begin to waver. Your eyes will be bigger than your stomach—your goals will be unachievable, and trust will waver in you as the leader, both internally and externally.

For instance, Army stakeholders would include soldiers and officers, civilian workforce, the local community, fathers and mothers who provide their sons and daughters who serve, and public service leaders all the way up to Congress and the president of the United States. In the commercial realm, stakeholders range from coworkers, subordinates, and all levels of leaders; to contractors, vendors, and suppliers; to customers and third- or fourth-party providers.

Whatever degree of contact the stakeholder has with the organization, you must link together these roles in order to give them a clear understanding of what you're trying to achieve, a purpose for what needs to get done, and the resources needed to get the job done. This requires trust and transparency, collaboration, and a collective responsibility. And leaders assume this responsibility.

Building Trust

Building trust is key to conveying organizational values, purpose, and goals; your people must know that the leaders in their organization—from their team leader to the highest senior leader—are going to take care of them.

Building trust with all stakeholders begins by understanding what you are trying to achieve. This means really knowing yourself through honest reflection. Why are you doing what you are doing? Whatever your reasons—family, community, financial, or other—there isn't necessarily any right or wrong in why you make your decision if you have trust and transparency with stakeholders. Once you understand what you're trying to achieve in your purpose and goals, you have the framework you need to align the organization with those goals and to make the best decisions.

Starting with understanding yourself is not being selfish. If you don't start with yourself, you're going to find yourself struggling constantly to achieve anything. Why? The more you understand yourself, the more you'll understand how you relate to everyone else and what you are capable of. Only when you understand what you're trying to achieve as an individual will you comprehend the sacrifices you're willing to give to achieve a certain goal.

It's difficult for many people to understand the magnitude of sacrifice when it comes to leadership. Often they see someone achieve something, and they feel they should be able to achieve it just as easily; they don't understand all the hard work that went into achieving that accomplishment. Leadership is a lifestyle choice that takes commitment and discipline; simply showing up every day does not translate to success.

Your internal and external stakeholders will commit to you as a leader when they recognize that you're responsible for your own actions and for their actions. You set the tone that creates a culture of trust. The way to do that is by setting the example through words and deeds, by making values-based decisions based on a key set of values that are understood by everyone within the organization.

Dan Morgan:
The Moment of Recognition

When terrorists attacked the World Trade Center in New York City on September 11, 2001, and we were put on a "war footing," my unit—the 101st Airborne Division's Screaming Eagles—was sent to invade Iraq. We were one of the first units that crossed the berm between Kuwait and Iraq into combat.

We were still at Fort Campbell, Kentucky, preparing for the mission, just days away from leaving our families and going into the unknown—another doorway while chasing the white rabbit—when I realized that the world had changed. Now, for the first time, I experienced a wave of emotions because I knew I was with an organization that was perfectly aligned to my values, goals, and purpose.

We were trained and equipped, and I thought we were ready to fight.

But standing in front of over a hundred soldiers who were about to go off to a faraway place—and maybe make the ultimate sacrifice—is when I realized that I was exactly where I belonged. It really hit me that I needed to be responsible for others more than any other time in my life and that the responsibility also applied to my soldiers' families remaining in the United States. These soldiers were about to follow my orders into combat knowing full well they could be killed.

But it was at that moment, on that field, that I realized that I was on the right path within an organization. It was the alignment of our Army values that is embedded within tough training, daily decision making, creeds and mottos, and other reinforcing mechanisms that enabled me to have the confidence to lead and make decisions.

I vividly remember standing in front of soldiers in formation on a field located in Fort Campbell, Kentucky, within a week of boarding a plane to invade Iraq. Everyone was nervous and excited to do what they had been training for months and years. Standing there, I told them they were ready and that I would be there every step of the way and would do everything I could to ensure they could fight and win.

I also said I could not promise that no one would be wounded or killed, but I was confident that everyone would fight to win and protect each other.

They cheered, and we shook hands as we each filed past each other.

I loved that day.

David Morgan:
A New Direction

After falling short on my grades in college, which prevented me from entering medical school immediately, I decided to build up my credentials by taking on a variety of jobs in the medical field.

One night, while I was still in my twenties, I was standing in the hallway at Georgetown Hospital with one of the pediatric fellows, and she was discussing a child who was very sick. They were trying to get him to another hospital to get treated because his health insurance only allowed two referrals, and Georgetown was the second.

I vividly recall the doctor, who was only a few years older than me, saying, "If this kid doesn't get to another hospital tonight that is better set up to help, he's probably not going to make it." He had been fighting his condition for the last several weeks and just wasn't getting any better. The doctor had exhausted all she could do and needed him to be transferred. The boy was being denied simply because of someone following some corporate decision on insurance policies.

I stood in the hallway looking at this poor child, who could not have been more than ten years old, lying in a bed with all sorts of tubes and wires hanging off of him, my gaze only interrupted by people passing between me and him. I thought of the potential future that may never be simply because of a number on a policy that some underwriter made. The creator of the policy had no clue who this child was and would never know him or his family.

My singular vision for the past several years was to help others. Up until this point, I felt that I could best achieve this vision by becoming a physician. Through this harsh experience, I learned the stark reality that my singular vision was not so singular. Becoming a physician also meant adhering to managed clinical care guidelines, hospital policies, and insurance company denials in cases where it was determined by someone other than me that my patients did not meet medical necessity criteria and were deemed "ineligible" for the treatment that they so deserved. The precious little boy fighting for his life taught me something very special that day. Indeed, helping others was still my vision—this experience gave me the insight and courage to correct this course that I had been on for so many years to realign my values, purpose, and goals with another pathway. Little did I know at the time that this pathway would be circuitous, oftentimes challenging, and continuously fulfilling.

That's when I realized I didn't want to spend the rest of my life in medicine; I didn't want to spend the next decade of my life going to medical school only to have an insurance company decide what was going to happen to my patients. That, I knew then, was not aligned with my values, purpose, and goals; I wanted to be a doctor because I wanted to help others. But after pursuing a dream for so many years, I finally reached the point where I knew I didn't want to sacrifice the rest of my life where much of my decisions were going to be driven by someone else. I wanted the ability to make an impact and change on my terms, at least as much of my terms as I could control.

So I had to gather the courage to admit that it was okay to take an alternate path. After spending the last decade of my life telling everyone that I was pursuing my dream to become a doctor, I had to come to grips with why I was walking away, why I was leaving a path that I had identified with for my entire adult life. It was a lesson that a profession does not define you, but your values and purpose in life define the job that you do.

That new path turned out to be enlightening for me, and it thrust me into an arena of responsibility that changed my life. The ensuing journeys brought new opportunities and experiences that I would never have encountered. I had the opportunity to make real, impactful change at a number of organizations; was fortunate to travel to places and meet people all around the world; and had profound experiences with a great group of people that will always remain a part of me. All of this due to the little boy in the hallway, so many years ago. I am forever humbled that his determination to fight gave me the courage to make the decision to pursue my dreams.

CHAPTER 2

Speaking Truth to Power

"'Speak when you're spoken to!' The Queen sharply interrupted (Alice). 'But if everybody obeyed that rule,' said Alice, who was always ready for a little argument, 'and if you only spoke when you were spoken to, and the other person always waited for you to begin, you see nobody would ever say anything,'"

E ven as a young girl, Alice had the good sense to consult with—and listen to—her Wonderland acquaintances Caterpillar and Cheshire Cat in her nonsensical Wonderland world.

In pursuit of their own white rabbits, great leaders listen to their team to understand and promote values-based decisions. They build trust in the organization by permitting people to speak opinions and challenge ideas and assumptions. That trust also means that team members know and respect your final decision and own it as a team.

This concept is difficult to grasp: As a leader, you don't need to know everything, and you must be humble enough to learn with the team. You must learn to listen and adjust and to give ownership to the team. You must recognize that people at all levels of responsibility have good ideas.

Speaking truth to power within an organization is about allowing and building in people the moral courage to speak their thoughts and opinions regarding an issue, idea, option, or anything of value affecting the organization. It requires you, as a leader, to understand the viewpoints of others first before you start providing direction. If you disallow free thought, you run the risk of creating an environment of mistrust that fosters poor critical and creative thinking.

Too many leaders do this inadvertently, and some are just narcissistic and drive their own solutions for their people to complete.

But if you do not build the courage in others to challenge you, you're failing them and violating your own values, purpose, and goals. You're stifling the team and hurting the organization and ultimately diminishing your capacity as a leader.

It used to be that the dynamics of the workplace involved more ingrained worker/boss-type strata: You listened to your boss, there was a lot of respect for authority, and you followed what authority told you to do. It was just part of the culture. But in recent years, there's been a leveling, or flattening, of power in an organization; more people are willing and able to speak up because they feel they have a voice. Facebook, Twitter, LinkedIn, Instagram—through these social media outlets, everyone feels they have a voice. This can be both a benefit and a challenge.

As a leader, you must have a twofold sense of moral courage. Naturally, you must be able to defend your organization and team against any and all spoilers. You must have the moral courage to stand up for what you know or think is right. But you must also allow and encourage your team to have the ability and courage to stand up to you and offer their opinions even when they run counter to your own. If you stifle that, you build dissent, and those who should be following you will weaken trust in the organization. This can quickly create fractures in an organization, especially in today's dynamic, stressful environment.

This is why you must empower people to speak truth to power in a dignified, respectful manner, where they know it is safe to do so—this demonstrates trust and transparency, collaboration, and collective responsibility.

Willingness to Resource as Needed

Building trust as a leader also means you must ask people to do things within their capabilities or provide them the additional resources they need to get the job done. If you ask someone to do something that's beyond their capabilities because they lack the resources needed to accomplish the task, then you will break trust with them. Instead of making yourself part of the solution, you're demonstrating to them—and ultimately to everyone else in the organization—that you do not care for them or for the organization.

As the leader, you must be willing to resource problems accordingly, including getting your team members any training they need to handle the problem. If you don't do this, you're violating, not promoting, the organization's values, purpose, and goals. You're setting the organization and your team up for failure over time. Turnover, climate, ethical violations, and so on result from breaking trust with your stakeholders—the people you serve.

This also applies to putting people in decision-making positions when they are not properly experienced, trained, or equipped; placing someone who's unprepared in a decision-making position is putting the organization at risk. People must be afforded the opportunity to succeed or fail and ultimately learn. However, you owe them the proper supervision so that they may develop as leaders. In business, very bad decisions can end in financial ruin—for a large business, that can mean millions of dollars; for a small business, it could mean bankruptcy. In combat, lives can be lost, which is acknowledged as likely, but lives should not be lost because of poor risk management and leadership.

This does not mean you should not challenge people to develop and assume more responsibility. You must push your people to overcome challenges and succeed while owning the risk of their performance. How? Be engaged, ask questions, talk to them about their methods, and engage them by incorporating their new ideas. This will help you develop your team. By talking to your team, you'll discover what unique experiences or skill sets members have and what training or additional resources they need.

Humility Is Key

Creating an environment of openness will require you to adopt a sense of humility.

This can be a challenge when you're often in environments where you're supposed to be the person in charge. Often, though, even in those situations, you may not know if you have the experience or knowledge to make the right decision—in other words, maybe you're not the smartest person in the room. In a situation like this, you must be humble enough to learn alongside your team. If you do, you will most likely make an acceptable decision, although it may not achieve the best results. But at least you are learning, and that is success.

Even when you are the most experienced person in a situation, you can still learn from others who maybe have more tenure than you, who work more closely with the task at hand, or who can simply offer an outsider's point of view. People will respect you if you ask them to explain things to you in the simplest terms; then you have the responsibility to listen and learn.

Also remember this: In any given situation, other people in the room are likely also going through their own developmental stages. They, too, are likely being thrust into an environment where they don't entirely know what they're doing. By creating a dynamic where there is open, frank dialogue, organizations will benefit from a better-informed decision.

Humility presents the biggest challenge for leaders today. Information comes fast, new technologies emerge, and people want solutions right away. So leaders increasingly make many problems urgent and simply spoon-feed solutions, which lack critical, divergent thinking and increase odds for negative long-term impacts on an organization and its goals. And this style of leadership fails to build strong trust and can lead to a poor climate and employee turnover.

Along with humility, controlling emotions can be a real challenge for leaders. It's too easy to base decisions on emotions, and while it is a mistake to be too emotional, caring and understanding can go a long way when making decisions. Being self-aware about your behavior, you can keep your emotions and arrogance, or over confidence, in check, which enables your humility

Passion, compassion, and anger are three emotions that are key for leaders to understand.

- **Passion** is showing enthusiasm for people and your work. Passion is not excitability or hyper-reaction to any challenge. You must be able to have fun. If you align your values, purpose, and goals with those of an organization, passion comes naturally. For some personalities, this can be hard; but regardless, you must find ways to show your passion. Passions comes from just being a present and positively engaged leader.

- **Compassion** is listening to people with empathy in order to help understand the problem and other perspectives. As a leader, you need to shed assumptions and compartmentalize distractions so that you can give 100 percent to peoples' problems or concerns. If you can do this, you'll build trust and enable success. When sitting down to listen to your team (whether they are soldiers, first responders, or business professionals), you must serve and give to them, not take.

- **Anger** is one letter away from "danger"—a very insightful quote used often. Anger tears apart trust. Make no mistake, the greatest of leaders lose their temper. In combat or other tense situations that have left you sleep deprived or at tremendous risk, you'll naturally become stressed. However, the outward display of anger over frustration can lead to violation of values and the disintegration of trust, particularly if it is a pattern. A technique to mitigate this risk in emotions is a disciplined schedule, and someone who helps point out when you are losing self-control and need a break or sleep. This takes discipline and humility to manage yourself.

The key to making decisions without injecting emotion into the equation is to pull back and think through the problem and then make a decision, which can be very difficult to do in a crisis situation. People can quickly get overwhelmed, and orders can get lost in the commotion. If you let emotion take over very quickly, you will lose control. You do not always have to make a decision at the table in the exact moment. Step back and see if they come up with a solution, or come back at a later time after your reflection.

Similarly, leaders who let emotion rule their decision making tend to have less control over their organization. It's a little like "The Boy Who Cried Wolf": If you're the kind of leader who is screaming and excited all the time, eventually that demeanor becomes background noise and followers won't listen anymore. By the same token, a completely emotionless leader may not be taken seriously when the need arises. If you speak in consistent and clear tones, you will be heard loud and clear when a matter of urgency arises.

Ultimately, as the leader, you must put the ego aside and not overreact to circumstances that alter or negatively affect your plans or decisions. You must remember that the organization is also everyone else, not just you. A leader's character in these times defines him and the organization. Leaders must constantly remind themselves that they are part of something bigger.

Dan Morgan:
Getting Back to the Basics

Every organization needs to be a learning organization; without learning, an organization will never discover its true self.

As an infantry battalion commander in the 10th Mountain Division, I was becoming exceptionally frustrated with the number of leadership and organizational assessments that our soldiers and leaders were required to do. It was exponentially challenging "to gain understanding of our climate," and eventually, and eventually the soldiers were numb to the value of the surveys.

We used a solution that was not necessarily unique, but it was effective. Every six months—four times over a two-year period—I gave guidance to my squad leaders and above that I wanted them to use index cards to provide me with input: "Give me three positives and three negatives about our battalion and three positives and three negatives about my leadership, and then submit those cards back up your chain of command."

The cards were submitted to my adjutant, who was instructed to mix the cards up, not sort them into specific units.

Then my command sergeant major and I grouped the cards into common themes: organizational positives and negatives and individual—my—positives and negatives.

Names of those who submitted the cards were optional and were only on a few at first. However, the last time we did this feedback and learning technique, more than 80 percent were submitted with a soldier's name, demonstrating an environment where soldiers had the moral courage and confidence to speak truth to power.

When I surveyed the cards, I found that they revealed some failures on my part—either in words or actions. If a particular soldier was involved, I went directly to that soldier and either apologized or explained why I said or did something. If it was a common situation, I would speak to the entire battalion—all 750 soldiers—so that there was a shared consciousness and level of understanding across the entire organization about what was said or done. Sometimes that meant apologizing to the entire unit for my failure or error.

Finally, I sent an email to all stakeholders—my leaders, peers, superiors, *and even my wife*—sharing with them what was said about the battalion and what was said about me. I focused on the three to five trends of weakness in the organization's systems and my personal leadership. I revealed the negative comments about me, and I explained what I was going to do to improve. I was very transparent about where my failures were, based on their comments, and I gave them a road map for corrective actions that I expected them to hold me accountable for. It was my contract to them. I was the deliverable in my service to them.

I learned that I am responsible for my failures and to my stakeholders. I learned that trust and transparency extend beyond your stakeholders. It goes further: it lands in your lap as a leader, and you must have the humility to learn about your shortcomings and failures. The hard part was acting on those weaknesses and ensuring they saw me taking action on those specific feedback comments.

David Morgan:
Dealing with the Spoiler

I was taught from a very early age that you should try to always respect authority, and that is still very important to me today. But when I was coming up through the ranks in the fire department, the biggest challenge was a senior leader of the organization, several years older than me, who was respected by the older generation.

Over the years, I rose in the ranks of the organization and eventually became recognized as one of its next potential leaders, representing the new generation, which had new thoughts and new ideas. During that time, this senior leader publicly despised me. He constantly berated me and challenged me, and he disrespected me at every opportunity. One of his tactics was to look right through me when I was trying to explain something; he viewed me as being beneath him, unworthy of acknowledgement. It was the most frustrating and, at times, the most degrading experience of my life.

Regardless, every day, I showed up for work because I had the moral courage to stand up for what, in my organization at the time, was my generational belief that what he was doing was wrong and that the vision of where he was taking the organization was wrong and that there was a next generation of leadership that needed to come in. At the same time, the older leader was placing so much pressure on me, I was constantly being prodded by my crew to step up and defend them. This went on for several years.

Then I became the chief, but that didn't change anything. In fact, his behavior became even more intense, because then he was the past chief—the retired ex, the old salty dog. He was granted status as a "life member," which in a volunteer fire department is effectively like tenure, where he was essentially untouchable as long as he did not break the rules.

The way the organization worked was that on the street it was very paramilitary, where orders and direction stood fast without debate, but everything inside was done by political consensus or by swaying the membership's position. Getting volunteers motivated required constant encouragement because if they lost interest, they would just leave. So it was a constant dance of trying to moti-vate and encourage while holding the highest standard to performance because mistakes could literally impact lives of our crews and the citizens we served. Having an obstinate, argumentative personality constantly criticiz-ing and challenging everything I said was counterproduc-tive—and that's putting it mildly.

Finally, one day we sat down behind closed doors to talk about an issue that was around before I became the chief, and he was a different person to me. He relaxed his gruff personality, and he was respectful, thoughtful, and sup-portive in what we were trying to do.

He still didn't agree with me, but after our conversation, our relationship changed somewhat. He knew I wasn't going anywhere and that I had won over internal and external stakeholders with my consistent focus on taking the high road, ensuring my performance standard was the highest I could muster from myself and my crew, and simply showing up every time I was supposed to.

Believe it or not, I respected the man throughout it all. He was a good chief in his day, but we just had two com-pletely different styles of leadership and beliefs in the organization's future. He was fiercely loyal to the orga-nization's past legacy, and I was making change for the future. Eventually, I found out that he actually respected me for having endured all the abusive behavior, making it to chief and continuing to lead through all the challenges that were put before me and defending the organization through it all.

And that's what I learned to do: Over time, I learned to fight for myself, for my team, and for everyone in the organization who was trying to propel us forward. During this time we were able to add new level of autonomy and responsibility to the department, addition of new service apparatus, new special operations capabilities and numerous capital infrastructure improvements, while along being one of the busiest volunteer departments in the United States.

Because of the members of the organization and the belief in our goals, we have since been able to accomplish what nobody in the organization at the time thought could be done.

In order to lead, you must develop the confidence and will to fight every day. Although leadership is about people, in the end, it comes down your own will to stand in the face of adversity. There will be failures and successes. No one can teach you the energy it takes to get back up when you are knocked down. That is one of those experiences you must live through to learn. It does not get easier with each time. However, you do know that you will be able to get through it and that it only temporary. Your success as a leader will be directly related to how well to react to adversity and how strong your will to achieve your goals when the spoilers try to bring you down.

CHAPTER 3

Bring Expertise to the Table

"'Be what you would seem to be'—or if you'd like it put more simply—'Never imagine yourself not to be otherwise than what it might appear to others that what you were or might have been was not otherwise than what you had been would have appeared to them to be otherwise.'" —The Duchess

Alice's adventure in chasing white rabbits was filled not only with constant physical change but also situational change that challenged her character and who she was or wanted to be. The more she learned about the whimsical Wonderland, the less she knew.

As a leader, your expertise will constantly be challenged as you chase the white rabbits that pop up in your world. In dealing with these challenges, you must know what your duties and responsibilities are and be an expert in those duties and responsibilities. As you develop in your career you inevitably will become responsible for leading team members that are much more capable in their roles. You do not need to be an expert in all of them, but it is imperative that you develop an understanding of how the organization functions. This does not require you to be a technical expert in all that your team and organization does. Rather you must understand what decisions you make, how your decisions impact action, and who they involve.

Your organization expects you to come to the table prepared to make a decision or give guidance based on your understanding of your duties and responsibilities and the problem at hand. Come to the table as an expert at your job, and it will build confidence in those around you—it is about competence. Even if you are not an expert on day one of your job or new role, through study and experience you will get better at your job and gain more competence.

To become the best leader you can be, you must balance carefully what you read with what you experience because what was relevant in the past may not be relevant today. There's no cookie-cutter approach to leadership; it all depends on your perspective and how the information you encounter is confirmed or denied, relevant or irrelevant. You must be willing to shed assumptions and not be anchored in biases from your past; remember that even similar situations from the past can result in different outcomes in the present or future. You will look back in time and think of things you said and did that you would never do again, but at the same time, you were 100 percent committed to your approach based on those circumstances.

Our advice: Leading in crisis will end and result in lessons, so embrace feedback as a gift and lead everyday as you were given a second life—another opportunity to serve others.

In many ways, leadership is about survival, and the better you know your own values in your job, both from reading and doing, the better prepared you will be. Leaders must fight every day to be better, to ensure that values, purpose, and goals are met in order for themselves and their team to advance. In this environment, performance is critical. But if you believe in what you are trying to accomplish, you live with a heightened sense of awareness, and that becomes a survival skill you use in making it through each day. The more intense the experience, the more intimate and memorable it becomes. This develops expertise in you and your organization, spreading competence and confidence across the breadth and depth of your organization.

Remember: When you make a decision, it's the best decision you can make with the resources and knowledge that you have in front of you at that point in time. If you become selfish or complacent or become less than engaged in making decisions, you become a risk to yourself and to your team. Competence and confidence will wane, and what follows is the breakdown of trust in you. If it's easy for you to make decisions that impact your team in a negative way, or if you don't have a tangible interest in the pain or the risk that you're creating by your decision, your presence at the table becomes a risk for the organization.

Leadership is an evolution; it's not a simple formula that works everywhere, every time, with everyone. You must be willing to learn, adapt, and modify all the time. Yes, you can read books about it and you can be trained in it through management courses and programs, but until you actually lead yourself, until you experience it, you're never really going to appreciate what it takes.

You can also learn leadership—good and bad—by witnessing it in others. As you evolve as a leader, you can consider different styles of leadership. But they must all be firmly rooted in the foundation of values, purpose, and goals of the organization. The leaders that bring expertise to the table are the ones who have aligned the values, purpose, and goals and know their responsibility to serve others in order to achieve success for the team. Good leaders bring expertise to the table on behalf of the organization, recognizing they are part of something bigger than their own self. But great leaders not only possess an expertise, they are also agile and adaptable to other perspectives—by being able to listen and adjust for better solutions.

Listen and Adjust

Bringing expertise to the table is a must for great leaders; without your guidance, your organization will wither. But great leaders bring this expertise to the table and adjust to input from other stakeholders who are trying to contribute a solution to the same problem.

There's a tendency for leaders to discount solutions or ideas from other leaders or stakeholders in the decision-making process. It's not always possible—or necessary—to get everyone's input, but better decisions can often be made when you take the time to hear what people crucial to the decision are saying—whether they are new to the organization or an experienced member of the group—and then to assimilate their point of view into any discussion on the matter.

If you can't identify the problem with a common understanding, you will likely have a disconnect among the team and a wrong or incomplete solution. A very simple example of this would be if everyone is analyzing a problem involving a coffee cup in the middle of the table but only the people on one side of the table can see that it has a logo, then discussion about that cup will be describing two different problems.

Collaboration over a problem can be especially difficult for leaders with a "take-charge" attitude, who often are ready to just make a decision and move on. In an era where there is such a demand for fast, impactful decisions, leaders often don't take the time to listen and adjust by understanding the positive or negative impact of their decision and others' perspectives.

So you must be quicker to listen and slower to speak instead of always dominating the conversation, because when you, as the senior leader, begin to speak, everyone else goes into listening mode and the options being presented cease. You get more respect and more credibility by listening, engaging, and allowing the conversation to take itself to a point where you and other decision makers or stakeholders understand—from a common point of view—the problem that you're solving.

The risks, however, are that you may dilute your own ability to make a decision; for some leaders, this dilution occurs to the point of always looking for someone else's input. It's also time consuming to listen and adjust, and after all the effort, you may still have people who feel excluded even when their input wasn't necessary for the decision.

So you need to use the listen and adjust concept judiciously, and when the situation doesn't allow for you to do so, you need to be able to explain yourself. For example, in situations where timing is critical, such as in combat or a tactical emergency, there obviously isn't time for debate and negotiation, and you must make an immediate decision based on the organization's values, purpose, and goals. But after the fact, at some point, you need to be prepared to listen to a dissenter's point of view and explain your decision. Good leaders take the time to do this.

At the end of the day, no matter how much dialogue occurs, the reason you're the leader is that you're responsible for developing the best option so everyone can move forward together as a team with a feeling of ownership.

Dan Morgan:
Calm amid Chaos

Although I trained to deal with loss of life, and I understood it, I didn't cognitively grasp the significance of it until I was truly faced with the potential loss of the lives of soldiers based on decisions that I had to make.

One night in Iraq in 2003, I had sent one of our platoons out on patrol to search for some black market criminal activity in an area I had responsibility for. I trusted my leaders, and risk was acceptable, so I chose to remain at the command post monitoring everything on the radio. This was very early on in the conflict, before we had armored vehicles that could take huge blasts from improvised explosive devices. Also, we didn't know at the time that the insurgency in Iraq was beginning to brew around us. But I did after this night.

While the platoon was on patrol, maneuvering their vehicles in very restricted alleys with no light except our night

vision, insurgents organized themselves on the rooftops overhead and began shooting AK-47s and throwing homemade grenades down onto soldiers in open
vehicles.

Explosions rocked the alleys and echoed two miles
back to our command post. The soldiers dispersed out
of the vehicles and returned fire. Some were wounded,
one gravely. I began hearing the radio reports of enemy
contact, which initially didn't cause me much angst. But
as I listened and started visualizing the environment
they were in—night, constrained alleys, the enemy in an
advantageous position on the rooftops—I realized that it
was more than just sporadic gunfire and that our soldiers
did not have a full grasp of the situation. Not only were
they managing casualties, but they lacked the combat
power to regain the initiative.

My first sergeant intuitively mobilized our quick-reaction
force as I tried to visualize the situation. Simultaneously,
our quick-reaction force platoon leader had developed
a route and was prepared to depart. When we arrived a
few hundred meters from the firefight, I saw with my night
vision an alley full of smoke, muzzle flashes from the roof
and the ground, and intersecting lasers from our soldiers'
weapons firing upward to the roof tops. They were caged
in, and if our first sergeant and quick-reaction force had
not taken initiative, I am not sure what would have been
the outcome. The sound was deafening, as automatic fire

echoed off the walls of the city and smoke billowed out of the alley.

One of the vehicles had been disabled in the attack, and a leader of the platoon had backed his truck back into the alley—which was still under fire—to retrieve a soldier who had been gravely injured; the injured soldier was the driver of the now-disabled truck, where a grenade had exploded in the floorboard, destroying one leg below the knee, severely damaging the other leg, and leaving his body filled with shrapnel.

With his truck bumper-to-bumper against the disabled truck, the team leader scrambled across the vehicles under fire and retrieved our wounded soldier as the other soldiers—all of them wounded with shrapnel—returned a barrage of fire to the rooftop insurgents. Simultaneously, we had fired illumination rounds behind the enemy so we could silhouette them and employ our sniper from our position.

The team leader realized our wounded soldier was losing blood quickly, so he grabbed wire off a rickety telephone pole and tied a hasty tourniquet around his leg—this occurred early in the war, before we were supplied with premade tourniquets. Meanwhile, another soldier hooked up the disabled truck to his truck and pulled the wounded soldier and truck out of the kill zone. We refused to leave the enemy any of our damaged equipment. He did not have this right.

By then, crowds of concerned and curious Iraqi citizens, along with suspicious people and cars, had begun to fill the intersection, and though we had broken contact from the insurgents, we could not get our soldier out of the area to take him to the combat hospital. The medics were working on him in the back of a truck while other leaders—some of them wounded—moved into position to protect the medics. I directed another platoon to clear buildings above us in order to prevent enemy sniper fire or observation.

Amid this managed chaos, a moment of calm emerged: as I was surveying our situation, I turned and saw the bloodied and dirtied face of our wounded soldier; his eyes had a look of panic. I bent over, placed my hands on his cheeks, and calmly said, "Hey, it's Captain Morgan, your commander. You're going to be fine. Just relax and do what the medics tell you. We're going to get you out of here, and everything will be all right." I believe this serene moment was not a conscious one but one of leadership built among teams in an organization that was aligned in values, purpose, and goals. We served each other. I saw a sense of calm come over that soldier amid the chaos, and for me a laser-focused sense of purpose. I had overseen leaders gain control of a violent, chaotic combat scene, and now, it was about getting our soldier out safely. It was about shared values, purpose, and goals reinforced by trust among people.

It was that eye contact with my soldier, another human being and young man with his life in front of him, that made me realize at that moment the significant responsibility I had as a leader.

Ultimately, we executed a high-risk, urban, aerial medical evacuation for the soldier because we could not maneuver vehicles anywhere. As a matter of fact, as I was requesting the evacuation, a 101st Screaming Eagle female pilot's voice came over the radio and said, "Where are you? I'll do it." I cannot thank her and everyone else enough.

It was a dangerous pick-up zone in the middle of an urban area at night and in an intersection with only feet to spare between the helicopter blades and surrounding poles and wires. But even though the enemy has a vote in every combat situation and people can make mistakes, I was confident we had the area secured and that no one would expect a helicopter to drop in. The pilot was able to navigate in and pick up our soldier. We all shared common values, purpose, and goals—so much so that everyone was willing to risk their lives for one another that night and for many more to come.

David Morgan:
Tunnel Vision

When people get excited or during tense times, people get what is known as "tunnel vision." This is when all of your attention is so focused on one thing that you lose sight of the big picture. Imagine looking through the end of a drinking straw. You miss out on everything other than what you see on the other end of the straw.

Everyone has this tendency when emotions get intense, but this can be incredibly dangerous to you and everyone around you.

In the fire service, there is an emphasis on the basics and not getting overly focused on one thing or solution. For example, we got called countless times to scenes where we had to gain access to cars or structures, and people would begin beating or prying on a door or breaking through a window, only to have someone come and grab the door handle and simply open what was an unlocked door. People easily jump to conclusions and go on automatic and miss out on the basics.

I can remember so many times where losing sight of the big picture almost met with disastrous results. I remember responding late one night to the scene of an accident where the car crashed into several telephone poles. Walking up to the car, all I focused on was the wreckage of the car with the power lines across the road and the car. I was trying to assess what was going on and began creating courses of action in my head of what to do next.

I blocked the road with my chief's car, which had enough strobes that it looked like a over-lit Christmas tree. I got out of my car and put on my gear, including my coat, helmet, and gloves. I grabbed my portable hand-held radio and started to give out orders to the crew. Working around downed power lines is incredibly dangerous. You cannot see the electricity and have no idea if the lines are charged. There are countless stories of victims, including firefighters, who have gotten too close to a line with horrendous consequences, such as having a finger or limbs simply blown off. Even getting shocked from electricity traveling through the ground from a nearby downed power line can produce such devastating outcomes.

As we realized that we had several patients still in the car, I started calling for more units on the radio and giving directions on what we needed to do to get the patients to safety and then to the hospital.

As the operation was progressing, I felt a slight rub on my helmet and did not think much of it, as we still had patients in the car. The rubbing became more annoying, and I tried to waive my hands and pushed away what I thought to be a limb from one of the downed trees. Eventually the rubbing became more annoying, and my helmet started getting pushed off my head. I finally decided to step back and saw I was rubbing against the downed lines from the poles that were wrapped up in the limbs.

Not only were the wires over the car and the road, but there were wires still in the trees, and in the dark I did not see them and walked right into them. As I regrouped I realized that the wires rubbing my helmet were only telephone lines but only a foot away were the high-voltage power lines that had been ripped down from over a hundred feet away. If I had taken another step toward those lines, who knows what would have happened. To this day I have no idea if those lines were active, but that instance has made me hypervigilant to focus on the big picture at all times.

I was focusing in on trying to do everything right and was too focused on only the chaos of getting the patients out of the cars that I lost sight of the basics. I was only one small step away from becoming another victim at the scene where I was there to help. In approaching all decisions, you need to take your time, observe the entire environment, and make deliberate choices. Many times people rush to judgment and focus on only a small portion of the problem, which appears to be the most dramatic. They lose sight in a rush to make a decision that they create more damage to themselves and others. Compelling yourself to look at the big picture is your responsibility as a leader.

CHAPTER 4

Perfect Information Never Exists

"Soon her eye fell on a little glass box that was lying under the table: she opened it, and found in it a very small cake, on which the words 'EAT ME' were beautifully marked in currants. 'Well, I'll eat it,' said Alice, 'and if it makes me grow larger, I can reach the key; and if it makes me grow smaller, I can creep under the door; so either way I'll get into the garden, and I don't care which happens!'"

Like Alice trying to navigate Wonderland, sometimes leaders hot on the trail of a fast-moving white rabbit don't have all the information they need to make a decision, but they must make a decision anyway. With the Internet and smartphone technology, we literally have a world of resources at our fingertips. But even with these and other tools available to us today, there are times when you are not going to be able to get your hands on all the information you need to make a decision in a timely manner. If leadership was a science, everyone could do it.

At times like these, it's up to you to make decisions with an understanding of the risks involved. Great leaders never leave people owning the risk; leaders own the risk. Organizations that have built the trust to speak truth to power and have the requisite moral courage among its people will stand up for what they think is best, particularly if the staff believes a leader is imparting too much risk through his behavior or decisions. Great organizations possess excellent risk management practices and communicate the risk among all stakeholders, but great leaders will assume the risk once the decision has been made.

Managing Risk

Chasing white rabbits will constantly lead you through doorways into the unknown. And whatever decision you're making as you step onto unfamiliar turf, in a sense you're managing risk—you're weighing outcomes and the probability of survival. In the military, of course, that takes on a more literal meaning—decisions determining a certain course of action in combat may result in loss of life. But it's also important when the survival of a business, and the welfare of the people that work there, are at stake.

Risk management in today's environment is often directly related to the information available; the number of actors affected; the consequences of your action or decision; and the behavior, actions, and decisions of those actors after your decision. It is a action, reaction, and counter action paradigm that you must accept as a leader. In today's fast-paced world and the global connectivity of people and cultures, information is often unknown or not readily available. And decisions cannot always account for every effect on every actor. Sometimes, leaders cannot wait and must decide. Often, in the time it takes to analyze a problem and get 100 percent awareness (and/ or consensus), the events surrounding the problem have changed, so not only are you faced with a new problem to solve but you've also lost the opportunity to make the most impact on the original issue you were trying to resolve.

So the challenge for leaders is to know when you have enough information to be confident in making a decision and letting the team execute the solution. You must be confident in situations with minimal information and ever-changing dynamics. Confidence doesn't mean that you know what the outcome of your decision is going to be; it's an understanding that you must make a decision, adapt to changes, and live with the consequences.

This is often complicated by the knowledge that your decisions are not always going to please all of your stakeholders; this is where trust and transparency create a shared consciousness about values, purpose, and goals. You must continually keep stakeholders informed and explain any risk across the breadth and depth of the organization.

In managing risk, leaders must get accustomed to the idea of being uncomfortable; constant discomfort will drive you to be better at what you're doing. That discomfort comes from accepting the fact that there are always going to be unknowns. In the military, those unknowns typically involve a combat situation with an often-unpredictable enemy. In the commercial realm, you're dealing with a shifting market environment over which you have no control.

In either situation, you can't afford to waste time wringing your hands and fretting about what to do, which way to go, what answer to give. You will be left behind, and your organization and its people will lose trust in you as a leader. You cannot roll up your sleeves and get to work if you are constantly hand wringing and nay-saying. That is just weakness.

It's like a fire department answering a call; from a tactical standpoint, the only solution is to take action. In other words, if the house is on fire, the house is on fire, and you can only stand around thinking about what to do for so long before the house starts to be irrecoverable.

When the alarm sounds in the firehouse, you never know if it's going to be a cat stuck in a tree or people trapped on the fifteenth floor of a high-rise building. These things are out of your control; but even in a wait-and-react environment like a firehouse, training and experience should kick in when a decision needs to be made.

One of the most difficult things you have to do as a leader is to make a decision without knowing the potential outcome—you must decide what to do without a complete understanding of what's waiting on the other side of an unopened door. Even if it's a decision that you make year after year, there is always the possibility that there will be a different outcome because of external factors beyond your control.

The way to combat these unknowns is to understand as much as you can about the environment that you're in, know what resources you have available, and explore any potential outcomes; this kind of analysis is an ongoing, constant requirement for leaders. Leaders must always ask themselves "what if?" Too often leaders get caught up in the race to take immediate action on information presented to them and on "next-on-the-agenda" items. Like Alice's frenzied white rabbit, they think, "I need to go to my next meeting," "I've got to read and respond to the next email," and so on. But leaders need to balance this sense of immediacy by continually assessing the environment and gaining experience in order to be better prepared to make a decision and possibly lead through crisis. This skill is about managing risk.

Types of Risk

When dealing with risk, there are a number of factors and levels to consider in making a decision.

The four factors to consider when dealing with risk are:

- risk to the force (soldiers, staff, team members, etc.);

- risk to the mission (the goals, values, and purpose);

- risk of inaction (making no decision on the matter, which can be okay); and

- political risk (elected officials, higher-ups, external stakeholders, etc.).

Understanding the four factors of risk and the impact on your organization's values, purpose, and goals enables leaders to make a decision. Without considering the four factors of risk, you'll find yourself outside an appropriate decision space, resulting in a wrong decision or inadequate options for a decision that can cause failure, loss of trust among stakeholders, or a significant setback. These negative consequences can have devastating impacts on progress, or forward movement, and may require external help to recover your organization.

If you don't cognitively acknowledge that perfect information never exists, you may find yourself increasing the level of risk in a mission because you've waited too long—a lost opportunity that could have catastrophic consequences. This is a message that bears repeating: At some point, you must make a decision, and then you must live with that decision, even if lives are at stake.

One weight on the shoulders of leaders today is that there are so many unknowns. In the military, for example, the enemy and tactics are very difficult to detect; enemy soldiers don't wear uniforms like they did in past wars; they blend in with the civilian population, and their weapons are often hidden and difficult to detect. With today's technologies—satellites, unmanned drones, and other sophisticated tools—it would seem that the military should be able to see, hear, and understand everything. That's simply not the case.

There is just so much information available out there that if you take all the time to analyze it, information becomes the objective rather than achievement of the goal. And in firefighting, the military, and law enforcement, people get put at risk. In combat, when enemy forces are conducting activities that clearly display hostile intent, meaning that they aim to kill or wound our soldiers or innocent civilians, military leaders have the moral justification within the laws of war to take action and kill the enemy, even if not engaged in direct contact.

That in and of itself is a hard decision to make; not only are you about to take someone's life, you may also be risking the life of your American or coalition forces, and you may destroy infrastructure in another country, which will have tremendous political risk for the host nation. This can be the most difficult doorway to enter when chasing a white rabbit. But you will learn.

While the unknowns are not as life threatening in the business world, the fact remains that the restraint that you need as a leader is paramount, but you must be sure you're making the right decision all the while knowing that perfect information does not and will not exist.

Dan Morgan:
Weighing the Risks

We were in Iraq, and my commander was on leave, which left me with the onus of responsibility.

We had destroyed a bridge because it was on a road the enemy was using to move large car bombs into Baghdad. Our senior leaders feared that the impact of these car bombs threatened our mission. Hundreds of innocent civilians were dying, which was sapping the will of the Iraqi people—and the public opinion of the United States. These large car bombs were moving through our area, and we needed to limit their routes and canalize them onto specific routes so that we could end this horrific mass casualty weapon.

The bridge was destroyed and reinforced into an obstacle. We could not watch over the obstacle with soldiers twenty-four hours a day, and if a contingency arose we had to come off this position to meet other requirements. Unfortunately, the situation demanded that we had to clear the area each time we reoccupied the area. This meant our soldiers put themselves at risk by patrolling an area rife with snipers and improvised explosive devices in order to make sure the obstacle remained effective.

One day, a helicopter pilot reported that the obstacle had been dismantled and the bridge had been haphazardly reconstructed and was being used again. We didn't know whether the bridge was still being used to move car bombs, but we knew there was still a very high threat of that type of activity occurring. So I made the decision to send a patrol to the bridge to identify whether it was passable or needed to be destroyed again.

My subordinate leaders disagreed with me because they knew it was high risk and that the likelihood of receiving enemy contact was high. There was an established pattern in how the area was cleared because of the restricting terrain of farmer fields and canals. Based on guidance and our mission, I weighed the risks to the force, received additional overwatch support, and gave the order. I still question my order to this day.

They patrolled on foot down to the bridge, and when they reached a place where they were forced into a single file, the lead soldier stepped on a dismounted improvised explosive device. The platoon leader quickly tended to the soldier, placing tourniquets on his two legs and one arm that had been blown off in the blast. Although the aerial medical evacuation arrived timely, the soldier died of his wounds while being transported to a medical station.

That soldier's name and incident is etched in my memory along with a vision of how the events unfolded—what I asked those soldiers to do remains with me to this day.

Looking back, I am not sure I would make the same decision today. I am not sure why. I know that perfect information would never exist on the matter. Did I listen well enough to my leaders who knew that terrain area better than I did? Did I balance risk to force and mission and risk of inaction with the political risk well enough? I had balanced the risk to the force and to the mission and thought we had provided adequate support capabilities. We had a mission, and the bridge was considered strategic in nature due to the destruction and death those car bombs were causing in Baghdad.

I think I had weighed the factors of risk and believed that the risk was acceptable. But did I give my leaders enough weight in my risk management? What about the risk of inaction? Would it have mattered at all if we had done nothing? I do not know. It would be like proving a negative. But I wonder if I gave due diligence to risk management for our soldiers, and did our leaders at headquarters own this risk? It is a tough situation and question. I do not know now. But as a leader, I will forever own this risk and live with the consequences.

David Morgan:
Emotion-Based Decisions

For a number of years, our company worked with a specific customer in the Army on a cutting-edge technology program that had never been done before. When the customer's program manager moved on to another project, a new program manager came onboard, and as a result, the program came up for recompetition.

At the time, we had enjoyed tremendous growth as a result of this program; it was really the first program that brought a lot of growth and recognition to our company, and it was then our primary business. What had started as me sitting in a small office near the Pentagon turned into a group of seventy-five people reporting to me.

When it came time to recompete, we thought we were in great shape since we had created the program and were the incumbent contractor that had all the knowledge and experience. We had a long-standing relationship with another company that was our teaming partner on this contract. They had access to the contract that the government was using to execute the work and we provided all the services and support to make the program work. We had developed a strong professional relationship with the customer and our teaming partner. The program was a great success. How could we not get the contract again?

However, while preparing for the competition phase of the recompete, our teaming partner informed us it was taking over the entire program and any future participation on our part would be severely limited. In other words, our teaming partner would be in charge and make all decisions, and our future involvement would only be on a case-by-case basis.

We were aghast and furious—we felt betrayed. We had taken a program that no one cared about and built it in three years into a program that was gaining industry relevance and importance. Almost everybody currently in the program worked for us, and walking away from the table would potentially mean at least severe staff cutbacks. Worst case, our company would be bankrupt, and each of us would potentially lose everything we had, including our homes. Our partner on the other hand, had no institutional knowledge of or investment in the program. They had everything to gain: money, power, influence. Our business ideas, our financial and intellectual investment, and even our identity were now in the middle of a hostile takeover—by the same people that were supposed to be our friends and partners; everything we had made was going to be taken away.

So we had a decision to make: Should we break ties, walk away, and try to win the business back ourselves? Or should we stay with the existing structure, potentially cut personnel, and be at the mercy of someone else for what could turn out to be piecemeal business with no real guarantee? If they were going to show us no loyalty today, we figured they wouldn't show it in the future either.

My head and my heart were conflicted over the decision; my head said stay, my heart said go. My thoughts raced over the trade-off. The old adage "a bird in hand" seemed logical—we should go with the new program and take what scraps we could get. On the other hand, we had built the program, and we should defend it at all costs.

Ultimately, my father and brother voted to break ranks and walk away, and in the end I "went with my heart" and voted with them—a decision I think of to this day. We decided we would try to compete with another team that we could trust better than the one that we had been working with.

But we lost that bid and were pushed out of the program that had been so near and dear to us. Several months later, we received additional information that our chances of winning back the program were nil unless we agreed to team with our original partner. Had I "gone with my head" and we stayed onboard, we would have landed another program that would have tripled our business; we still would have been in the game. So it turned out that a slice of the pie would have been better than nothing.

Fortunately, nine months later we landed another major project that kept the company afloat.

In hindsight, I've learned to be more cautious in gambling on my emotions. But sometimes the only way you learn is by making the tough decisions and by trusting your instincts. Even instincts, however, can occasionally be wrong, and you have to deal with that failure. You must make the tough decisions on a regular basis in order to learn to be more confident in your own decision-making process.

PART TWO

What Do We Do Now?

"'But,' said Alice, 'the world has absolutely no sense, who's stopping us from inventing one?'"

Like Wonderland, today's work environment is a place where fixed perspectives and personal sense of order collide with constantly shifting boundaries; seemingly logical strategies that worked in the past are largely illogical in today's world. Based on the new paradigm, there is an ongoing requirement to challenge yourself as a leader in order to maximize performance of your team and yourself. It's like you have to develop a sense of clairvoyance. And that is hard with a multi-generational workforce!

Through our experiences, we've discovered what is important for leaders in today's workplace is that we must continually adapt to a changing paradigm, while putting people first.

We've recognized that the new workplace has multigenerational leadership and that everyone with the organization is there because they are aligned or discovering their alignment with an organization's values, goals, and purpose. As a leader, you will ultimately begin to recognize who you are and what you're a part of; you are likely also beginning to notice that things often don't make any sense. You're trying to get your hands around your leadership in order to be successful and achieve the values, purpose, and goals that have been established for you.

In order to prevent yourself from being overwhelmed by the rapid pace of change with everything that's available to you and how your organization is dealing with all these new inputs and threats or concerns to your organization, you have to take the initiative to say, "Who's stopping us from inventing a new one?" If your organization needs to change the way you do things in order to be relevant and succeed, then you have to figure out as a leader what you need to do now.

Part of that is bringing together varying levels of multigenerational leadership under a shared consciousness or understanding of how you're actually going to achieve success and remain relevant, not only for your own well-being but for the well-being of your organization and the people in it.

There are three chapters in this section, in which we introduce the concept of the "Three I's": innovation, inspiration, and inclusion. Our "Three I's" are approaches in how leaders can best align multigenerational challenges in the workplace with an organization's values, purpose, and goals.

CHAPTER 5

Innovation

"Alice opened the door and found that it led into a small passage, not much larger than a rat-hole: she knelt down and looked along the passage into the loveliest garden you ever saw. How she longed to get out of that dark hall and wander about among those beds of bright flowers and those cool fountains, but she could not even get her head though the doorway; 'And even if my head would go through,' thought poor Alice, 'it would be of very little use without my shoulders. Oh, how I wish I could shut up like a telescope! I think I could, if I only know how to begin.' For, you see, so many out-of-the-way things had happened lately, that Alice had begun to think that very few things indeed were really impossible."

Alice's "out-of-the-box" thinking helped her continually escape the predicaments she found herself in after chasing the white rabbit. Just ask the gardeners, Two, Five, and Seven.

In order to be relevant when chasing white rabbits in today's environment, leaders need their organizations to exercise that same kind of "anything-is-possible" thinking. We're talking about innovation at all levels, not just technology. There will always be another way to accomplish a goal or improve performance. We believe this is the driving force for any organization; in being innovative, it needs to be relentless, creative, and critical with regard to how it's looking at its people, products, processes, and procedures in order to succeed.

This requires a new mind-set where you, as a leader, feel you are completely liberated to be different and to employ new ideas and concepts that can be translated into capabilities that allow you to succeed, regardless of your responsibility. And it involves what we mentioned earlier—trust and risk management. It must be acceptable to try something without the fear of being fired, even if it turns out differently than you hoped for.

Only by building trust and transparency, collaboration, and collective responsibility within the organization will you be able to foster new ideas through divergent thinking, and bring out the best performance and creativity that you need to succeed.

Trust Your People

Whether on the battlefield, firehouse, or in the boardroom, your team must follow your orders, even though they know failure—or even death for a soldier—is a possible outcome.

To do that, your team must trust that the orders you're giving are values-based and ethical. If you can build that trust as a leader, whatever level of leader you are in an organization, that trust is going to allow your people to take the necessary steps to achieve the mission assigned to them.

To be successful as an organization, you must always push to be better, and the only way to do that is to build a culture that is free to express ideas. Even the smallest idea—maybe just a piece of an internal process that is viewed as insignificant—can make a major impact to how an overall organization progresses.

You also have to allow your subordinate leaders and the team to stumble at times, but be proud of the fact that they're taking the steps to innovate, to challenge themselves, and to challenge the organization to get better.

To be innovative, businesses often have to reinvent themselves: What does the company offer? How does it pursue new markets? How does it keep the competition at bay? And at the core of that continual push is often the reuse of technologies and skill sets for purposes outside their original intent. For example, software created for use in gaming may ultimately be used for warfare simulations, or surveillance technology used to secure a nation's border may ultimately be used in training sessions. Drone technology and video technologies developed over the last ten years of work in Afghanistan and Iraq are now being used to help train NFL and college football teams by creating complete situational awareness and analysis of the field. The technologies enable coaches to assess what happened in a play—where people moved, where they were looking—and can give rapid feedback to players on how to perform.

By allowing conversation to evolve, an organization can spring-board time and again into new markets, processes, and areas of business that propel it forward.

Engaging and Providing Direction

Even though some ideas fail, you must have the motivation and courage to continually try. After all, failure often isn't the result of bad ideas but of bad execution.

Everyone in your organization contributes to the team. A lack of contribution by any individual member is a failure of all parties; it's a failure of the leader, it's a failure of the other team members, and it's a failure of the member that's not contributing. There is no single point where a person can't contribute; someone may not be competent in a particular area of a problem that you're trying to solve, but that doesn't mean they can't contribute.

Often, innovative people and concepts are easily dismissed; leaders don't really engage, and they don't provide positive reinforcement to people who step forward to look for something new. Many times this is because leaders are just trying to make decisions and keep things moving forward as efficiently as possible, with minimal disruption and no risk. Any change is filled with risk and uncertainty that will take time and energy from the task at hand.

But there's a large percentage of the population that comes to work every day, and they're looking for something bigger than them-selves to believe in. If you can't get them oriented to look for new opportunities to improve, to look for new challenges, you're losing out on their ability to contribute to what might very well make a major difference in your organization.

As the leader, you must solicit feedback and ideas. You must understand opportunity may come from anywhere and anyone; sometimes the person that has the least technical knowledge is the one that has the most commonsense approach. You must have a sincere interest in what your people are trying to achieve at all levels, which can be a real challenge as ideas progress and get more complex. If you engage, if you visit with people inside and outside the organization, you'll foster trust, initiative, and a desire to succeed for the welfare of the organization and each other.

Innovation is also about having an idea, experimenting to prove it out, then either altering the idea or investing in it. Agile teams are very good at doing exactly this sort of experimentation and changing direction based on the results. Agile leaders are able to actually look into uncharted or unknown situations and then bring willingness and confidence within themselves and others around them. Leaders carefully construct the environment for people to grow—and to break through the physical and mental limits of what they do on a daily basis—in order to allow them to be innovative. How do you do this? Visit them and listen, and let them give their idea a try. True innovation works without boundaries. However, successful innovation comes about when the team is aligned with the organization's values.

Building an innovative team includes recognizing innovative ideas and rewarding people for the courage they're demonstrating. Avoid "hope-based leadership," which skips over validation or assessment. At the end of the day, most people just want recognition for what they're contributing to the group.

You must also remember that the fastest way to kill innovation is to take somebody else's idea and take credit for it. When that happens,

CHASING THE WHITE RABBIT

people will cease to step up and contribute ideas for improvement. Instead, recognize the achievements and efforts of your people with something as small as a personal thank-you or a heartfelt face to face or just looking them in the eye and saying, "You've made a difference."

Debunking "The Squirrel"

The idea of chasing the white rabbit is also about people running from rabbit hole to rabbit hole and becoming distracted with what the real goal is.

Today's environment is rife with distractions, creating new navigational challenges for organizations.

For example, multigenerational leaders are entering the workplace with varying levels of understanding of technology and a lack of experience in this diverse environment. Their struggle is to connect themselves, their workplace, and the people who look to them for leadership to a long-term, sustainable vision, despite the fast changes and demand for information and solutions.

The challenge is what is commonly known as "the squirrel." Imagine driving a car and someone suddenly yells "squirrel!" As the driver, you would tense up and look around for the squirrel you're about to hit with your car. It's a problem you're dealing with, suddenly, right then and there.

In reality, a squirrel is very small. If you hit it with your car, you'll experience little, if any, damage, although you would likely kill the squirrel. However, there's a chance the squirrel would run underneath the car and not get hit, or it might turn around and go back to the other side of the road without presenting any sort of threat. The squirrel represents a situation that seems to need immediate attention but in reality may not require a lot of attention or require you to take any action at all.

It's similar with technology today. People easily get enamored with the information that is provided to them, and a lot of leaders seem to believe that they must react and solve a problem right away. The reality, however, is that often whatever is being presented to you might be irrelevant or might simply be an idea for the future, not this moment.

Make no mistake: You need to react in times of crisis. But living for the day-to-day decisions without planning for the future creates unnecessary stress in the organization. There is no reason for leading through crisis day to day. Leaders, instead, need to replace a crisis-based, reactionary mind-set with visionary, proactive thinking. This will guide the team, while building competence, confidence, and collaboration.

Again, one of the biggest challenges you must deal with is when and how to make a decision when you don't know all the parameters that will impact the decision you're making. This is especially true when it comes to technology; there's no way you can stay engaged with all of the developments on the horizon, but you, as a leader, have to be able to understand when an opportunity is presented to the organization. This requires trust and transparency while you as a leader can listen and adjust to your people.

So when you're chasing rabbits, be careful of the "squirrel!"

Appreciate the Larger Context

A lot of people want to build a foundation on the present because that's what's comfortable to them—they don't like the ambiguities of what tomorrow may bring, so they want to stick their head in the sand rather than chase a rabbit down a hole. But if you can create a framework with the organization's values, purpose, and goals, then as technology evolves, your organization inherently will evolve with it. You shouldn't have to change your values and purpose, and possibly even your goals, based on an evolution of technology.

Amid a dynamic shift that is making it difficult for leaders to follow the old paradigms, how does a leader leverage technology and existing infrastructure to communicate the vision of the organization to stakeholders? This is one of the biggest issues facing organizations today; they're trying to use technologies that aren't suited to their needs, they're trying to use something that's old to express something that's new. This diminishes the impact of the message.

There's a tremendous desire to look for consultants or tools to fix problems that are, at their core, mainly about people. Using tools to make people better is a dramatically different approach than helping to make your people better by equipping them with the right tools. Technology is little more than an enabler; people are still the solution to today's challenges.

Investing in people is going to give you a far greater return than investing simply in tools; technology is going to come and go, and by the time you learn how to use a new tool, another version will have taken its place. Why invest in a tool to solve today's problem when you need to invest in people to solve tomorrow's problems?

There's also a tendency for leaders to put people in charge of seeing their own ideas through maturation, but that's not necessarily the best approach. Instead, the skill sets of various individuals should be matched to whatever roles a project requires—proposal writer, project manager, and so on—which means the big thinker will rarely be in charge by the end stage of a project.

The hierarchical command-and-control approach to leadership no longer allows appreciation for the larger context of what's going on in the world. Our military faces this challenge today in a world of increasing and complex threats to stability and security. Simply because you're a leader doesn't mean that you must define the future environment and how the organization will move forward. If you're a big-idea person or a concept person, that doesn't mean you're really good at squeezing efficiencies out of a process. Both of these talents are innovative and future looking, but their horizons are different. Where one may be good at seeing into tomorrow, the other is better at looking into the next decade. Leaders must build a culture of delegation and collaboration to address the larger context of the environment in order to make the best decisions for the organization.

Recognizing the various skill sets in your organization and setting it up so you allow people to look at current challenges and future opportunities for your organization is key. You need people who are innovative today in the way they make the organization more efficient tomorrow. The person who's going to be operationally effective today can be very innovative and forward thinking, for example, in figuring out how to maximize the current use of mobile devices, but that's different than thinking of the big idea of what's going to replace the iPhone or Android.

Again, creating an environment where all talents are appreciated is key to attaining trust and transparency, collaboration, and collective responsibility. Innovation is great but on its own is nothing. It needs what we'll talk about in the next two chapters: inspiration and inclusion.

Dan Morgan:
A Lifesaving Innovation

As a company commander in the 101st Airborne Division and part of the invasion into Iraq in 2003, we fought north to Mosul, occupied and built some operating bases, and started learning about the local area. We needed to find out who the influential leaders were, what the threats to stability were, and if there were any imminent threats to the new Iraqi government officials or to US forces.

Soon we began to receive intelligence that we should expect attacks in our area. We had done surveys across our area of operations; it was only three months after the invasion, and our leaders had developed surveys for our area of responsibility. Our sergeants and lieutenants had developed some innovative ideas on their own to help us understand what was going on. The words "insurgency" and "counterinsurgency" had been discussed but were not official at the time.

We discussed the possible threats to our forces, and one of the leaders suggested that we did not have sufficient means to do lifesaving care at the point of injury; we did not have adequate tourniquets and training. Since we were going to be in the area for a long time, he suggested that we purchase some one-inch-wide ratchet straps for every soldier to carry on their protective vests to use as emergency tourniquets.

It seemed easy enough to implement, and it made sense to do, so we went ahead and purchased the straps. Once the straps arrived, every soldier in the command had them on their protective vests.

Within a few days of everyone being equipped, the leader who had made the suggestion was on a mission. I was heading back to base, and he was heading out on that mission when we passed by each other at an intersection and an improvised explosive device went off under his truck. The explosion rocked the vehicle and threw soldiers onto the street. The vehicle rose up onto two wheels before settling and rolling to a stop. AK-47 fire and rocket-propelled grenades (RPGs) were heard almost simultaneously. Soldiers staggered about trying to shake off the effects of the concussion. Some fired wildly in different directions because the cracking of the AK-47s was echoing off buildings, making it impossible to pinpoint the direction of fire.

My truck was also rocked by the blast wave, throwing my driver into my lap. It took me a minute to crawl out and get to where our soldiers were. The leader and his truck were a mangled mess. After establishing security and clearing the kill zone, I moved toward the devastated truck. As I pulled some of the metal to extract him from the truck, I accidentally released pressure on his leg and discovered that he had lost a leg. And I inadvertently released a surging flow of blood.

That's when a combat medic in the back of the mangled truck suddenly lurched forward from the rear of the vehicle to where I was aiding the leader. Our medic reached down and grabbed and released the tourniquet on the leader's vest and swiftly ratcheted it down on the leader's leg. We got him out of the truck; he is alive and well and back with his family today.

The leader's innovative thinking had saved his own life, and it was a culture of innovation that had allowed his ideas to be expressed openly. This credit goes to the non-commissioned officer corps and our company's first sergeant, who facilitated "white board sessions" and after-action reviews after every combat engagement, regardless of its outcome. He wanted his leaders to learn and succeed. He saw that as their job as leaders. They had more trust and transparency, collaboration, and collective responsibility than I have seen to date.

What is even greater is that after this leader's injury, he took his experience and led technological advancements in medical simulation training, realism, and lifesaving techniques. Leaders like him have led an entire force to build the necessary skills to stop the bleeding in ways no soldier has done in past conflicts.

David Morgan:
Innovative Reuse

Our company, STS International, has been very successful in innovating. We've had to reinvent the company at least a dozen times: what we offer, how we offer it, and who our customers are. Many times we've been forced to evolve and innovate because the products and services we were pursuing, or the market segment that we were looking at, had moved past where we were.

At the core of these changes has been a continual push to use and reuse a set of technologies outside of the original purpose.

We started the company with two main product offerings in mind: developing support products to telephones that the government used for secret conversations and building software and hardware for medical simulations, which helped people train how to become better medical practitioners by developing their knowledge and skills via gaming technology. From there, we branched out to a number of other programs involving surveillance technologies, which included cameras, sensors, radars, and other devices; biometrics technologies (including eye scans, face images, and fingerprints, used to detect and identify people); ultra-protective body armor systems; highly trained field service support teams that could fix just about anything, anywhere in the world, with little support or notice; large scale database programmers; and, most recently, installing state-of-the-art satellite communications systems on military aircraft.

With such a wide variety of products and systems, we have been asked how we have been able to excel at diversity, whereas most companies try to be highly specialized in a specific area or technology. Some of it came out of sheer necessity—to put food on the table—but we are also very good at looking at a problem and leveraging new technology or approaches into a new way of doing business.

For example, when we first started in the medical simulation market, most of the training products in the market were leveraging computers to extend and support training with video games or interactive media. However, in medicine, the biggest training gap has always been from the classroom to the patient. The first time you need to do something under stress is typically with a real patient. Struggling with the need to create "near-real" training environments, we realized that the greatest challenge was the ability to create, record, and measure the training so the student could get feedback.

At the same time, we were heavily involved in developing mobile security surveillance solutions that integrated sensors and cameras, which tracked vehicles and personnel across huge spaces.

Then we thought, "Why can't we combine the two?" So we put the video surveillance technologies with the medical simulation software, and we created medical training and simulation systems that involve mannequin "patients" that react to trainee actions. These systems could be moved to the students via trailers and set up inside or outside to create dynamic scenarios that could be used to simulate stressful environments. For example, the military used it to control audio and special effects in recreating the sounds of battle. We would track students throughout the training and integrate it to scenarios that could be dynamically adjusted remotely by the instructor or by the inappropriate actions of the trainees.

We were able to take the lessons learned from developing mobile surveillance systems that were intended to autonomously observe and detect "bad guys" across vast areas and apply them intelligently to watch and assess students in small areas.

Although the concept started with STS leadership, the innovative developments came from staff performing assemblies and hardware integrations, the people doing the hands-on creation of the end product. To innovate you need to be open minded, challenge the status quo, leverage existing competencies and assets, and be bold enough to step up to voice your ideas.

Because we allowed that conversation to evolve, it allowed the company to springboard into a whole new business line that has continued to propel the company forward. We eventually leveraged this success and have gone on to do medical simulation products for the Army, Navy, Air

Force, Marine Corps, and others, where we have been involved in training tens of thousands of students. And we've done similar innovations multiple times throughout the lifespan of the company. We have continued year-over-year growth in a collapsing federal market space and have received numerous awards for innovation, all due to the willingness to try and being bold enough to say, "Why not?"

CHAPTER 6

Inspiration

"Alice was beginning to get very tired of sitting by her sister on the bank ... when suddenly a White Rabbit with pink eyes ran close by her ... Alice started to her feet, for it flashed across her mind that she had never before seen a rabbit with either a waistcoat-pocket, or a watch to take out of it, and burning with curiosity, she ran across the field after it, and fortunately was just in time to see it pop down a large rabbit-hole under the hedge."

What inspired Alice to chase the white rabbit and begin what ultimately became an epic adventure? It was not boredom. It was more than that. It was curiosity. It was thinking. Similarly, the fear of stagnation and irrelevance in the marketplace is what often motivates leaders to chase white rabbits in their efforts to drive their organizations to success. But this fear is not inspiration. Inspiration isn't what you have or who you are or what you are doing. It is what you think about it.

Inspiration is a challenging concept that requires the leader to discover his own strengths. How do you inspire in an organization that is faced with a dramatic and daunting pace of change? How do you inspire others to buy into an organization's values, purpose, and goals?

Organizational approaches that work for business do not always work for the military, because its ultimate goals are to win in combat and prevent the loss of lives. Businesses, generally speaking, focus on profit and productivity. Although these are important, watching the bottom line is not the way to inspire people in the military. There's no single approach that works every time.

On the whole, large organizations struggle to innovate and inspire people. Organizations that maintain a hierarchical or chain of command structure sometimes struggle to truly inspire people to innovate and take risks. But some of the notable organizations that have done this include Google, Amazon, and special operations in the military.

Regardless of an organization's management structure, leaders at any level can inspire people and initiate innovative change if they remain focused on their area of influence. They must be present and visible, engage and understand their people, and create a positive climate and culture.

Being Present and Going First

Few things are more inspiring to a team than following a leader who places himself on the line for an organization. Leaders risk themselves for others—in any organization. But teams who are inspired by their leaders will willingly follow them into any rabbit hole.

In the military, the leader goes first into battle; without leader presence, no inspiration would exist in the military. If he's not physically present, then troops aren't going to believe in what's being asked of them; soldiers need to believe that, whether wounded or killed, they will go home.

In firefighting, even when it's not required, the chief is often the first in and the last out of a situation. What's more inspiring than to see a leader exit a smoldering building just as exhausted as the rest of the team? What message does it send to the team when they see a committed leader getting his hands dirty packing up supplies or cleaning up apparatus in preparation for the next crisis?

Some leaders are born with a natural charisma, but that alone won't inspire people to follow; sooner or later, most people will see through the façade of that personality.

Being an inspirational leader requires you to create an environment of long-term learning, development, and growth for yourself and for the people who work in your organization. What this equates to be is rallying your people with your enthusiasm. But it's more than just motivating them to complete a task they've been given; it's about getting people to take responsibility for their actions and behaviors. The more you can develop your people to understand and respect their own responsibility in the organization, the easier it will be to build an environment where people are working toward your vision.

Leading from the front is a balance between being the leader and being a member of the team. The epitome of leading by example is taking on the responsibilities you would ask of someone else so that you can understand what you're asking. If you treat a job you're asking someone else to do as menial, then they're also going to see it as menial and not place importance on it, or they're going to feel that they are not as important as others in the organization.

Obviously, there are different levels of responsibility in every organization, and every responsibility level comes with professional education and credentials. But that doesn't necessarily mean that one job is more important than any other; for example, you can't open a door without someone there to unlock it. If you lose sight of that as a leader, you run a very big risk of having the organization not be in line with your ideals. Don't ask or seek luxury or privilege. People need each other. So, be present. Be a helper. Ask what they need.

So as the leader, you must be the role model for the organization; you must be present, relevant, and authentic at all times. In business today, there's little room anymore for the ivory tower, where everyone has a private office and sits at a desk overseeing others who are "beneath" them. Even leaders in senior management should participate and contribute in all levels of the organization.

Motivating with Big Ideas

There's no real magic in creating an organization's vision. It's just big ideas, and big ideas get people excited. Your vision, in essence, is the picture of what your organization should be. When your team has a vivid picture of the future, they're going to work hard to turn concepts into capacities and then into capabilities. They will be motivated to come to work, and they will be able to clearly communicate the big ideas of your organization.

In today's dramatically changing environment, you must immerse yourself in the organization to understand where your people believe it is today and where it should go in the future. You must do this by watching and listening and gathering information from everybody in your organization so that you can begin to paint the picture of its vision. This must be done collaboratively and on a personal level (not just by sending out an email to gather input or ideas). For example, join your team over the lunch hour in the cafeteria; sit at different tables and really talk to your people.

Once you've observed how others view the company and its future, then you must turn inward and reflect on your own values and the direction that you want to take the organization.

One of the most important things leaders do is communicate the vision for an organization—what vision are you trying to achieve, or what will be the ideal state for your organization when a particular goal is met? Communicating the vision is critical. Leaders must ensure that the story of what you're trying to achieve is explicitly understood by everyone, including internal and external stakeholders. To do that, you must understand the perspectives inside and outside your organization and refine the story so that all parties understand it, not just the senior managers or the board of directors. There will be people who will only understand or relate to certain components of your vision, which is why it's imperative that you express it in clear, relevant terms.

Effectively communicating your story happens by being present and engaged with people about what they're doing as it relates to the organization; be sure they know where the business is going and how they're contributing to the overall vision of the organization. Be with your people and listen to your people—don't just direct them.

Then you must record the vision on paper; make it short and simple and easy enough for everyone to understand. Leader engagement and presence reinforces vision. Simply putting a vision in writing is not sufficient; it requires continuous word and deed by you, the leader.

Once the vision has been documented, then it needs to be conveyed to the organization. This demonstrates that you were listening when you communicated with the team; you've taken into account their ideas and desires, and then you've reflected on the information.

After the vision has been released, you must continue to communicate it across the breadth and depth of the organization. That way you're building trust and transparency, collaboration, and collective responsibility within your organization.

Dan Morgan:
Never Underestimate Inspiration

For a time, I underestimated the impact that military spouses and families had on our well-being as an organization; I didn't truly appreciate what they provided our soldiers who left their homes to go fight in faraway, distant lands. I felt their environment and stresses did not compare. What I did not know is that I was breeching trust within my own family, because I discounted their situation.

During a combat deployment and within minutes of taking over the area of operations, we had a platoon out on a mission. Some two hours into the mission, these young men hit a devastating improvised explosive device that killed five soldiers. The bomb was over five hundred pounds, buried under the road. It threw the parts of the armored truck more than five hundred feet from the point of detonation.

One of the soldiers killed was a senior leader in our organization who everyone looked up to. He was a true leader, a role model who was always present with his soldiers. He was fearless and courageous, and he loved his soldiers, and they loved him. His loss, along with the loss of his young soldiers, placed the entire organization in a state of shock because he seemed invincible.

While he was a phenomenal member of a team, he was also a husband and a father, and his wife back in the United States was responsible for the welfare of the spouses and the families in that particular organization, which numbered more than 140 people.

In our organization, my wife was the senior spouse advisor. She had the experience of our previous combat deployments and losses behind her and knew this combat deployment was going to be worse. She had built relationships with these women over the months preceding the deployment, and they had developed their own training and special level of trust and love.

When our fallen hero's spouse was notified that her husband was killed and made the ultimate sacrifice, the spouses bonded together like nothing I have seen before.

This bond among those women enabled our fallen hero's spouse to remain committed to the welfare of the organization. She stayed on as the senior spouse at her own choosing in order to provide mentorship, guidance, love, and support for the family members within that company, despite the fact that she was grieving for her own personal loss.

We spent thirteen more months in combat and experienced dozens more wounded and fallen heroes. And through it all, this beloved fallen hero's wife remained as a steadfast leader in our organization; she inspired everybody around her and touched lives both inside and outside the organization with her unwavering courage. She still does this today for my wife and me. This love and commitment to each other is inspiration—a suffering and sacrificing in order to be a part of something bigger than yourself.

David Morgan:
Inspiring Self-Motivation

Firefighting and public safety are the epitome of a collaborative environment with one overarching mission—provide prompt, effective emergency services to enhance community welfare. On one cloudy Sunday afternoon, my squad did just that. The call came in around 2:15 p.m.—a report of a fire in an apartment building close to the station. Within minutes, our squad and the supporting stations nearby arrived on the scene—the building was pouring out dark, heavy black smoke causing zero visibility. The tension and excitement was palpable.

I was coming from a different direction, and as I approached the building I could see the billowing smoke from over five miles away. The two-fold goal was simple: save lives and contain the fire. The objectives to achieve the goal were complex, extraordinarily grueling, and very, very risky. As I arrived on the scene I met with my deputy chief, and we quickly organized teams to survey the entire apartment structure to ensure that all residents were rescued and escorted within a safe distance away from the structure—there was no time to decide which belongings they could take with them.

Although the entire building was engulfed in black smoke, we knew that the fire source was in the basement apartment, so without the ability to see, we were relying solely on radio communications. Containing a basement fire is a particularly delicate and dangerous task, as one step in the wrong direction could cause the floors above to collapse and, even worse, the slightest draft could cause rapid combustion; both outcomes were potentially fatal.

Then we heard the broadcast on the radio. Firefighters trapped in the basement! I looked at my deputy and decided that since he had the command post already set up, I would go in the building to take over the rescue. I took another team with me to contain the fire and protect the trapped firefighters. Together, we ran into the building, down the stairs, and into the black smoke and began the search. It was difficult to see anything. Going into a fire is chaos. It is not like the movies; there was fire raging over our heads and dark black smoke to the ground. You cannot breathe unless you are wearing a mask. There is so much noise with fire trucks, people yelling, radio transmissions, power tools, and even the sounds of your own breathing. You are so covered up in gear you cannot tell how hot it really is until it is almost too late.

We found the team in the back bedroom of one of the apartments. The ceiling had collapsed on them, and one of them had gotten trapped by all the ceiling debris and all the contents from the room above. Luckily on the crew was one of the best firefighters I had ever trained with. He was able to get everyone calmed down enough to get the trapped one out of being entangled. One by one we accounted for the crew and got them out of the building. I made sure to be the last person out of the building and that no one was left. It got very hot, very fast. I knew it was time to go. As I was running up the stairs to get out of the building, the explosion came seemingly out of nowhere. The fresh air created from the floor collapse fueled the flames and overtook what was left of the building. Physically and emotionally exhausted, I was able to get back to one of the trucks and account for the entire squad—the entire squad who, without hesitation and without question, risked their lives to ensure the safety of people they had never met. Without hesitation and without question, they listened and followed direction from their leader. Without hesitation and without question, these volunteers ran into a burning and severely compromised building to protect their community on that day without the compensation of one single penny.

As a leader of a volunteer organization, I wasn't able to rely on external forces (e.g., increased pay or bonuses) to inspire my team to perform beyond their potential or to show up every day and contribute to society or to collectively move with precision in one direction that lead into and out of a burning building. I saw tremendous potential in everyone that I worked with and could only rely on tapping into that internal motivation in each of them as inspiration. I did my best to create unique conditions for people to motivate themselves to succeed as a team. Some were called to spend time helping others with the satisfaction that you truly made a difference. Some were there for comradery and bonding with a team that you cannot get elsewhere. Others were inspired by being a part of something bigger than themselves and pursuit of even bigger dreams. Whatever that internal force is—with or without the carrot at the end of the stick—leaders will inspire action by taking time to truly understand the motivators internal to each of their team members. With this understanding, leaders can create an environment where team members can draw upon this core inspiration to succeed.

CHAPTER 7

Inclusion

"'Now, I give you fair warning,' shouted the Queen, stamping on the ground as she spoke; 'either you or your head must be off, and that in about half no time! Take your choice!'

The Duchess took her choice and was gone in a moment.

'Let's go on with the game,' the Queen said to Alice; and Alice was too much frightened to say a word but slowly followed her back to the croquet-ground."

In Wonderland, Alice ultimately chased the white rabbit to a place where not fitting in appeared to be a life-threatening matter. You, on the other hand, must not lead by intimidation, like the Queen of Hearts in Alice's world. Instead, as a leader, you must understand where each member of your team fits in and give him roles and responsibilities.

In order to drive an organization forward, you must have all three components that we discuss in this part of the book: innovation, inspiration, and inclusion.

The last of these, inclusion, is about having touch points where you reach out and relate to people on an individual level. People in your organization are doing great things, and in an environment where organizations span the globe, you must learn how to lead people differently.

Your methods of inclusion don't have to be incredibly profound, but you need to have a way of engaging with the people in your organization and having a conversation with them about what they're doing, what they're trying to accomplish, where they're going, and how that relates back to the organization.

Talent is more diverse than ever, with workers from a spectrum of cultures, generations, and expertise populating a workplace. All of this leads to a host of perspectives on any subject and on any project, creating unique challenges for inclusion. It is easy to forget about people and teams when the pace is relentlessly fast; decisions seem to be needed always, and diversity in the workplace appears to be counterproductive.

Often, information is created by the actions of others, and technology is exponentially surpassing many organizations' ability to change. As technology creates gaps in organizational communication, leaders must find innovative ways to attract, retain, and engage their workforce.

As your organization grows and you chase more and more rabbits, you're not going to be able to include everyone in every decision. But even if you're the CEO of a very large company, you need to find ways to make people feel included and to make them feel that their comments and contributions matter. Because no matter the size of the company, you still need everyone to be on the same page.

Servant Leadership

Building an environment of inclusion means you must figure out a way to harness the energy and skills of people and use technology as an enabler for people to provide solutions for the organization. The best way to do this is through servant leadership, which uses inclusion as a workplace strategy for success.

Servant leadership is people focused; it's about understanding that the people of the organization are the keys to its success. That success can't be measured by the outputs of goals and the objectives of a particular task at hand; it must also be measured by leadership and team development to enhance the well-being of the entire organization and the people in it.

Servant leaders must spend a great deal of time sharing what they learn and helping others through such things as career counseling, suggesting courses of action or ideas, and recommending new ways of doing things. Because they are giving and not taking, servant leaders are the beneficiaries of important contacts, information, and insights that make them more effective and productive. As a servant leader, you have more power and influence because the people in your organization will recognize that you're serving them—you're making sure that they learn and that they're helping each other to succeed, personally and professionally.

Viktor Frankl, a prominent psychologist and survivor of Auschwitz prison camp during the Holocaust, wrote that the pursuit of happiness is really a temporary state of being in which you are seeking and taking things to give you that sense of happiness. But where happiness is truly derived is through giving to others because giving back is what really instills meaning or a sense of purpose.

Since it is about being a habitual giver, not a habitual taker, servant leadership can be exhausting. But leading others and being responsible for others gives you a sense of purpose and meaning. This, according to Frankl, is the pursuit of meaning—by giving, you develop meaning. And while giving can be depleting and suffering, it is also self-replenishing. That is why we tell you that leadership must be a conscious lifestyle decision.

Too often, when chasing rabbits, we see leaders who drive their organization to quickly achieve goals and objectives pertaining only to a task at hand, and when all is said and done, their organization is burned out, unhappy because of all the continual taking—without giving—by the leader.

That type of leadership in today's environment is a recipe for failure. It's not how a successful organization builds inclusion to give people a sense of meaning and purpose. Ineffective leaders sit in a corner office, a cog in a wheel placing stamps of approval on paper that they then move on to the next desk. There must be engagement across the organization, both vertically and horizontally, to make sure that everybody is included in solutions, and it's your responsibility as a leader to ensure everyone understands that.

Being a servant leader is complex; at the same time you're giving guidance and instilling the vision, you're also taking input from staff and trying to ensure they have the tools and resources they need to execute and achieve goals.

People often think that the greatest job in the world is at the top, like being at the peak of a pyramid. But what they don't realize is that, as a servant leader, once you reach the pinnacle of that pyramid, it inverts, and then you're effectively at the bottom, balancing the entire organization on your hand and trying to make sure that you're keeping everything up and functional.

Under servant leadership, the "I" becomes "we" as another way of building inclusion. Successes are not about how "I am a great leader" or "I want this done." That kind of language is divisive; it builds walls between the leader and workers. Besides, everyone knows you're in charge.

The servant leader builds inclusion through language using "we." It's about us and how "we are striving for success" and "we are moving forward" as a team. This way everyone begins to increasingly share responsibility toward the solution.

But if things start going wrong and you have mission failure, the responsibility is all yours, the leader, because you're the one who's ultimately responsible for the team. At that point, it becomes an "I" problem, not a "we" problem. And as you take on that responsibility, you show the team that you take responsibility for failure.

Building the Team

Once you've built the environment where the sense of inclusion exists through servant leadership, then you'll be able to build teams to deal with specific problems or challenges. At any given time, you'll be able to build adaptable teams that will collaborate and bring different perspectives to the table to solve a problem.

Leaders need to break down barriers—the silos of parallel, noncollaborative thinking—that for so long have dominated organizational landscapes. Just look at American intelligence. In the past, before the September 2001 terrorist attack on the World Trade Center, intelligence organizations were prime examples of the left hand not knowing what the right hand was doing, because the structure of those organizations was not set up to share information.

In the military, for example, we speak of the "enterprise," or enterprise management. It is another system taken from a business model. So, every military staff section has built their own enterprise within the larger organization's enterprise, resulting in aggressive pursuit for results, or outcomes. The risk in this management style, and particularly large organizations that place demands on subordinate units, teams, or organizations who have lesser capacity, is that there is no one who can effectively ensure stovepipes of excellence, or "stovepipes of the enterprises," are being synchronized to a common goal.

As you build trust in your organization, you'll be able to break down walls and demolish barriers—"the stovepipes of excellence"—and enable collaboration between teams. And as you garner commitment from your teams, you will move from conversation to cooperation to collaboration and a collective responsibility.

Also remember that both internal and external stakeholders are part of the team, and that inclusion is about keeping everyone informed. Bringing everyone to the table makes it more stable, more trustworthy, and more respected.

Building, managing, and leading a team includes sharing your intent as the commander or business leader about what needs to happen when you're not around.

One door that many leaders dread opening is one of the hardest but most impactful tasks a leader can undertake—and one that will net more engagement from your staff. That task is training someone to be your replacement, which inherently is counterintuitive in most people's minds. Training a replacement is instinctual in the military. In the event that a leader gets injured or killed, or for some other reason is no longer available, someone has to take over the role and continue to move the troops forward.

But in the corporate world, leaders tend to feel that training someone else to do their job makes them replaceable, when in reality it allows them the time to focus strategically on the long-term well-being of the organization. This act creates depth in your role and more skill for the organization, it empowers the person that you're working with, and it allows you to migrate into another responsibility that will potentially propel your career along with the organization's overall success.

Training and developing someone else to do your job also challenges your perspective by inspiring yourself to raise the band of excellence within the organization and your leadership skills. More important, the process of training and developing leaders passes on both your institutional knowledge and your knowledge of the role. In addition to developing someone else into a leader, it also develops you as a leader because you have to become that much more consistent and confident in your own decision making on behalf of the organization's values, purpose, and goals. Consistency helps those people making decisions when you're not in attendance; by knowing where you stand on the organization's values, purpose, and goals, they will be able to make decisions that are in the best interest of the organization.

Ultimately, your responsibility as a servant leader is to ensure that the organization continues to exist without you. This can be particularly difficult in the commercial realm, where it may seem that you're diluting your own value by giving away all of your intellectual capital to a replacement. But inherently, teamwork is what builds an organization; if everything revolves around you, and then you leave, the entire organization will struggle.

Dan Morgan:
Building a Team

I had a boss who sat me down and talked with me about how to build a team by communicating vision and intent and letting your subordinate leaders find the solution. He told me this enables everyone to be part of the solution and take ownership: You owe them counsel and leader presence, he told me.

The way he explained this was by drawing a box on a piece of paper. "This box," he said, "represents my vision and my intent. The perimeter of the box represents the limits that I've narrowed my vision and intent down to, so there are some constraints and guidance that have to be adhered to. This may be directed by superiors or constrained by law or my assessment of risk to soldiers and the mission. But inside this box is where we're going to let our leaders operate and make decisions to solve problems."

Then he placed a small dot right in the center of the box and said, "Dan, this is the perfect solution. It might not necessarily be the best solution, but it's the perfect solution because I'm the guy in charge, and this is the way I would solve whatever the problem may be."

"But," he told me, "do not tell them how you would solve the problem." Of note, I still struggle with this today based on my personality. But I am learning to listen to the opinions of others.

Next, he placed a dot outside the box and said to me, "If your solution is outside of this box, would that be okay?" I replied, "No, sir, because it's outside of your vision and outside of your intent." And then he put a dot inside the box but way up in the far right corner, and he said, "Would this be acceptable to you?" And I said, "Yes, sir, it's within your vision and intent."

Finally, he asked me, "Would it be acceptable to me?" And I replied, "Uhhhhh, I don't know. I would hope so."

"That's right," he said. "If you were outside of this box, you would be fired or removed from your position for further development. But that would also be my failure because it's my responsibility to develop you through this problem solving by leader presence and counsel. That is how you will build your junior leaders and develop them to help us achieve the organization's mission. And they must stay within our values—always."

It was a phenomenal way to communicate with me; I understood how it represented the broadest limits and let me understand that we had a vested interest in each other's success. There was trust. Leaders must unleash their people to develop innovative solutions, while using values-based decision making, that are aligned with the organization. If you keep in mind the principle of inclusion—and you are present and listening—you will inspire people to be innovative for them and the organization as a whole.

David Morgan:
Taking Care of All Stakeholders

When working in a volunteer fire department, you can run so many emergency or fire calls that you get numb to the shock of it all. Out of several thousand calls a year, several hundred of them are the same types of calls; when you see similar events happen over and over again, they become sort of commonplace.

One day we were running a call for an automobile crash on a nearby highway. We probably run anywhere from ten to a hundred of these calls a week, and most of them turn out to be very minor, pretty straightforward.

This particular call involved multiple vehicles, and one of the vehicles was wrapped around a tree and had people trapped inside. It was a very horrific call, and three people were severely injured. But the team was very well trained, and the call went like clockwork.

When we were packing things up and leaving, I got very introspective and started thinking about what a great job we had done.

Then I turned around and saw a shell-shocked young man standing on the divider of the limited-access highway we had been working on. I went over to him, and after talking to him, I found out the details of the accident: He had been driving a car behind his mom and two sisters, who were in another car that was towing a U-Haul carrying his belongings; they were driving him and his things to college. The car in front of her had slammed on its brakes, and she had slammed on her brakes, and then the young man had braked. But when the young man braked, he skidded on wet leaves, slid into the back of the trailer being towed, causing it and the car that was towing it to jackknife and flip over.

So he was partly responsible for the accident that put his mom and two sisters in the hospital, and there wasn't any certainty that they were going to survive. This was baggage he was looking at carrying for the rest of his life.

I realized then that it didn't matter that we had done a great job in extracting everyone. My job was to take care of the entire incident, everyone who was involved, and that included this young man, a stakeholder in the accident.

At times it is easy to forget that the actions you take have a greater impact than you may realize. There is a natural desire to be drawn into the most intense, exciting or rewarding activity around any job. However too much focus on what may you see as rewarding or significant may ignore the other persons or parties involved. It was at this incident that I really understood the importance to evaluating the entire impact of my decisions and that you must be keenly aware of what is going on around you. If his mom and sisters did not survive, he was going to have to carry those memories for the rest of his life.

As a leader, you must always uphold the values, purpose, and goals of the organization. You must never get so full of yourself that you forget that your role is to provide the best resources to those people who are working for you, with you, or around you so that they can make that kind of impact on the next person.

PART
THREE

How Do We Do It?

"I can't go back to yesterday, because I was a different person then."

L ike Alice in the wake of her adventures, we've realized that we're different people than we were twenty years ago, and we're going to be different people tomorrow. We identified what we value in our lives and determined a purpose for ourselves. And we've accepted our lifestyle as leaders within organizations that espouse similar values and purposes. But as we chased the white rabbit, we have struggled through change or adaptation to the environment around us.

In the days to come, we must continue to adapt in order to overcome challenges and turn them into opportunities, and we must continue to drive our organizations even further with a sense of purpose and desire to succeed. This is responsibility placed in us as a choice because we love leading others to create a positive change in their lives and those around them.

The previous discussions in the book were about you, as a leader, creating an environment for a successful organization. Now we'll embark on a discussion about what you, as an individual, need to do to turn principle into practice and ensure success as it relates to the previous discussions.

We've identified three attributes that you need in your leadership kit bag: posture, positive pressure, and patience. These "Three Ps," as we've termed them, are not mutually exclusive, they are mutually reinforcing—you must have all of them to be successful. These will enable you to measure your own actions and develop programs that are good for your team and that help you and your team work together to build success.

CHAPTER 8

Posture

"Next came the guests, mostly Kings and Queens, and among them Alice recognised the White Rabbit: it was talking in a hurried nervous manner, smiling at everything that was said, and went by without noticing her…

Alice was rather doubtful whether she ought not to lie down on her face like the three gardeners, but she could not remember ever having heard of such a rule at processions; 'And besides, what would be the use of a procession,' thought she, 'if people had all to lie down upon their faces, so that they couldn't see it?' So she stood still where she was and waited."

I n the end, for Alice, instead of chasing rabbits, it made more sense to follow her own heart and mind.

While there are a number of meanings associated with posture, in this context it's about knowing who you are and what you're doing no matter what rabbit you chase, no matter what doorway you enter. As a leader, it's about how you hold yourself inside an organization, your presence and your position there, and how you reflect your own beliefs.

It's also about what people see when they look at you or interact with you, including their impression of you based on your words and actions. This stems in part from your decision making in a way that reflects your own values, purpose, and goals as well as those of the organization.

Most organizations have the values-based discussion—what are the values of the organization or the team—but as a leader, it's difficult to express those values without overlaying them with your own. This is a prime reason why it's essential for a leader today to align with an organization that reflects his or her own values.

Once you start laying out the values to the organization's stakeholders and then to the outside world, your decision making must be rooted in those values. Otherwise, it won't take long for people to call your values what they are—lip service.

If you allow yourself to stray from those values, to chase rabbits too far into the weeds—which is not difficult because leaders get tempted to do other things that are easier or more self-centric—then you must take a hard look at your decision making. Is what you're doing moral and ethical? Are you taking too much risk? Are you crossing an unhealthy line between your personal and professional relationship with an individual?

If you fail to delineate the moral and ethical boundary and ensure decisions are firmly entrenched in a framework that reflects the values of the organization, you immediately dilute your own ability to be perceived as a leader. You're perceived as someone who lacks confidence, who is self-centric or -serving, or who does not reflect the values of the organization.

In essence, you should always lead by example, and in that, be reflective of the ideal state that you want the organization to be. Anything you perceive you want the organization to mimic or replicate should be the focus of your efforts every single day. For example, if collaboration is an important component to solving your problems in the environment today, then you must create a very collaborative environment. And you must be part of the process throughout the entire organization; you can't just dictate to your people, "Go collaborate." Or if your goal is to inspire, you must stay in that mode at all times: You cannot allow your own passions, perceptions, or everyday emotions get in the way of being that leader. You've got to be able to, in each moment, reflect on your purpose and very clearly delineate the "whys" of everyday actions: "These are our values" and "This is what we're trying to achieve."

In short, posture enables you to walk tall within your organization and within yourself. It's a little like walking through a park and coming upon a large, wary, unleashed dog. If he senses fear in you, he may become aggressive. But the taller you walk, the more composed you are, and the more confidence you exude through your posture, the more likely he is to remain calm and go on about his way.

In an organization, your posture must also be in evidence during those times when you make a mistake; then you must acknowledge that you did something wrong and take responsibility for the error.

Maintain Rigid Self-Control

In order to present the appropriate posture, you must maintain rigid self-control. It takes a lot of internal energy to continually maintain the behaviors and actions that reflect upon the values you put forth. Without doing this, however, you're sabotaging your efforts; you'll lose the ability to maintain a cohesive vision of what you're trying to accomplish.

Posture is especially critical when dealing with a particularly fearful situation—for example, being on a battlefield. A military commander exhibiting panic in words and actions will cause soldiers to quickly lose confidence; they'll begin to feel like they're going to fail because they don't have confidence that you're going to make the right decisions or provide them the right capabilities to succeed in combat. Worse still, soldiers may begin to take things into their own hands to try to solve the problem, and as the pressure builds, start making the wrong decisions.

It's important to remember these points because running an organization is often about "managed chaos." You're trying to balance a thousand different things at the same time to make sure everything's being done effectively. But you can't allow that chaos to cause you to emotionally and intellectually make a rash decision. By having a solid understanding of yourself and maintaining self-control, you'll be able to consistently enforce your own decision-making process. A good example is a military saying, "Sleep is a weapon." It gives you rest and the capacity to deal with stressors better the next day. You could add working out and eating well to the sleep example as it relates to rigid self-control.

Posture is maintaining rigid self-control. Whether in a corporate boardroom or a military briefing, you must maintain rigid self-control of your own opinions no matter how strong they may be—especially when there are other strong opinions in the room. The key is to avoid destroying your credibility by losing control and launching or participating in an argument. The moment you raise your voice, you begin to create a divisive relationship, whether it be with your peers, your superiors, or your subordinates. Once you lose control, the things you say and do cannot be taken back, and it can take months or even years to repair the damage.

The Importance of Transparency

It's imperative to be open and honest with your stakeholders and your team to ensure they fully understand what is being asked of them, where you stand on issues, and how the organization is performing. This is a challenge for leaders: You must maintain self-control by masking your feelings, and yet you must also be transparent and let everyone know when a situation is serious and demands attention.

Make no mistake. Transparency doesn't necessarily mean that you are exposing all the facts of a situation; there are many times you cannot be completely transparent about your decisions or choices. For example, you cannot discuss the details of personnel decisions or some financial or business decisions, as that can create vulnerability or expose you to competitive threats. Transparency means that you are being as up front and honest as you can be without violating the trust and responsibility that you have to the organization and to your team.

In any organization, certain people typically have access to information that isn't widely disseminated to the rest of the company. But when there is information that is not meant to be common knowledge or widely dispersed, then it's still up to the leader to communicate that fact as opposed to avoiding a subject altogether or offering an overly abbreviated explanation. People can see what is happening in their organization, and they recognize when you're being dismissive. So while you don't always have to offer full disclosure or give away institutional secrets, you must be prepared to allow individuals in your organization to challenge your decisions and then be as transparent as possible about why a decision was made, or why information is not available to everyone.

Ten seconds is a long time. Stop right now and look at your watch tick away ten seconds. As a leader, you can make some serious decisions in ten seconds that help out your organization, especially in combat. However, to do this, a leader must have been transparent and fully engaged with his team in understanding the environment. A great technique when tempers begin to rise is to ask people to be quiet and look at their watch for ten seconds. Then look up and say that was ten seconds—a pretty long time. Let's relax. Let me explain myself. I have time. Then we can make a decision.

In other words, explain the "whys" when you can, and when you can't, tell why you can't explain. People in your organization would rather have some honest explanation than work in an environment where the leader operates in secret behind closed doors.

Dan Morgan:
Being the Example

During my last deployment to Afghanistan, I was in a video teleconference with my superiors when we started hearing some gunfire. I didn't know what was happening outside, so I asked a member of the staff to see what was going on. He came back and reported that there was a shooter on the base and we had one casualty.

We could not find where the shooter was coming from at the time, but the leaders reacted quickly and moved to certain force-protection locations and key strong points where we could pull security to protect soldiers as well as the command post.

Then I turned to the video teleconference and told my boss about the incident, that there was a suspected enemy shooter on base. My command sergeant major and I got up and put on our combat kit and went outside to see and develop the situation. We moved quickly to inspect appropriate positions based on past rehearsals. Gunfire was less sporadic but was still coming from the same direction. It was from a heavy-caliber machine gun. It didn't seem to be coming from a location on the base, but rounds were impacting across the base, and we were fortunate to have just one casualty thus far.

It would have been very easy for leaders to scream and run around in a panic trying to get control of the situation. But what I saw was captivating. Leaders were moving deliberately, checking on soldiers. Seeing this gave me pride and confidence. I followed their example and began making my way to as many soldiers as possible. I hoped, as their commander, I could reinforce confidence in the situation that was being developed by their immediate leaders.

After checking on our positions, we linked up our Afghan battalion commander partner and asked if he knew where the fire was coming from. At the same time, one of the soldiers identified the machine gunfire point of origin. Immediately and with zero hesitation, our Afghan partners deployed counter mortar fire against the enemy machine gunner, while I went to visit our wounded soldier. In the trauma room, I watched our medics treat a few casualties with precision, stern commands, and confidence. It was inspiring to see this among young leaders.

As a leader, maintaining rigid self-control in difficult environments is absolutely critical to maintaining your organization's confidence. The moment you begin to lose self-control in combat is the moment that you start violating laws of land warfare and making unethical decisions that can have a hugely detrimental, legally punishable impact on individuals. My ability was developed through a series of situations as a leader in combat, but the leaders I have had around me reinforced this ability. It was reciprocal trust and transparency among leaders that gave us organizational confidence to accomplish more than we ever thought we could.

But there is also a simpler explanation of what posture means. I was fortunate to visit the Pentagon with some of my peers where we had fifteen minutes with our chairman of the joint chiefs of staff, the most senior military officer in the US Armed Forces. We asked him for one straightforward piece of advice, which was: "If your soldiers don't want to be like you, I don't need you." That is what posture is about.

David Morgan:
Transparency Brings Solutions

Recently we won a big contract that no one expected us to win. We had no experience with the customer but felt confident we could execute the work.

In order to win, we had to co-opt the incumbent contractor who had the work because we could not do the work without them—they had the skills, capability, and knowledge that simply could not be replicated. We also had to bid really low, below the point of pain, and then hope everything would work out in the end. We put the bid together, cut the price, cut it some more, and then at the last second we cut some more; it was the most aggressive bid we had ever done.

I sat at home that night thinking … go big or go home; that's what we had done.

But weeks went by, and we never heard back, so I thought we had lost the bid. I was a bit disappointed but also relieved—it would have been a great contract, but it would have been high risk and a struggle to make it work for the price we had proposed.

Then I got the call. I was excited and scared; we were the little dog barking wildly in full sprint, chasing the bus down the street, and just before it was out of site we caught a hold of the bumper. Now what? Well, for starters, I celebrated with my team. We had accomplished something no one believed could be done.

After we signed the contract, we approached the incumbent contractor to give them the good news, and that's when the trouble began … they refused to sign up to work with us. They never thought we'd get the contract; they expected the government to award them a sole source contract. They were fuming because they were no longer in control and were going to lose the revenues they expected.

We needed the contractor in order to execute the work, but weeks of negotiating with them went nowhere. I reached out to the government to explain my position, but I was told the problem was all mine—I had less than fifteen days to get the program up and running or we would be in default.

Finally, the contractor came to a face-to-face meeting to try to negotiate a solution.

But their position was firm—and absurd—they wanted all or nothing, which the contract would not allow.

They thought we were stealing their business, so suffice it to say, the negotiations were insane: crazy demands, outrageous accusations, pounding the table. We were in an untenable situation—no middle-ground solution and an unsympathetic customer (the government) that was threatening breach of contract and termination if we could not resolve our differences. In the negotiation room, I remained calm, but at one point I was so upset I excused myself "to make a phone call"; as soon as I was outside the door, I just stood there trembling with rage, frustration, and desperation.

I went home that night exhausted, exasperated, and at a loss about what to do next.

The next morning, as I was getting ready to head back to the negotiation table, I thought to myself, "What do I have to lose?" I decided to just walk into the room and be completely transparent; no arguing positions, no trying to leverage advantage. Just lay all the facts on the table, don't give ultimatums, and answer every question as straightforward as we can, with all the information.

Once they understood the numbers and the facts from the bottom up, we asked them, "How would you want us to solve the problem?"

That was the breakthrough; they understood why and what we were doing. It took half a day to create a solution that was a win for everyone.

Once I stopped being so involved with the demands and brought transparency to the table in an effort to focus instead on a solution, we were able to move forward. Coming out of that experience, we have all continued working together and have gone on to do great things individually and together.

CHAPTER 9

Pressure

"Alice said nothing; she had sat down with her face in her hands, wondering if anything would EVER happen in a natural way again."

A t times, the pressures of chasing the white rabbit threaten to overwhelm Alice, at one point causing her to take pause and despair. Pressure is levied on people to achieve goals, but leaders must find ways to approach pressure from a positive state of mind. This does not preclude the requirement for reprimands or even dismissals, when necessary, but leaders must create positive pressure in an organization to ensure alignment of values, purpose, and goals.

As the leader of an organization, positive pressure demands your continual involvement because stressors and demands on people can lead to stagnation and cause productivity and high morale to collapse. At the same time, managing pressure also means having a balanced approach to peoples' well-being between work and family.

"Positive pressure" as we're using it here is not just about fixing the negative, avoiding punishments and accountability, or taking time off to recuperate. Instead, it is about standards and discipline, about applying the appropriate level of energy to an organization to achieve your next set of goals and reinforcing it with incentives and rewards.

As the leader, you're constantly putting directed energy into the organization to be able to create an environment where people will move forward. Without that energy, that positive pressure, people too often end up resting on their heels and the entire organization begins to get lax about what it's supposed to be achieving. Leaders must ask daily: "Where are we on the pressure scale? And what do I need to do to manage it better to meet our goals and protect our values?"

People tend to work better when there is a goal to achieve, whether it's winning a proposal, meeting a new sales quota, or reaching an ideal state of understanding. So how do you effectively apply the energy that you need to individuals, your team, and your organization as a whole to perform at its best? How do you encourage performance without going overboard with the amount of pressure you're applying?

You must determine the appropriate amount of positive pressure by using an outside-in view of what is going on. What are the business outputs of your mission? How are your people coping? What concessions do you have to make in order to achieve your daily, weekly, or monthly requirements? You cannot allow yourself to be drawn too deep into the morass of daily duties or your view will be clouded.

You must operate between a comfort zone and a zone of strain or stress. This requires a shared consciousness between you and your people. People need to understand your expectations, and you must help them achieve those standards. Overwhelming pressure that is not managed positively and carefully can create a toxic environment. This is why leaders must manage pressure accordingly, and that requires a careful attention to detail.

Taking Care of the Team

Applying pressure can be received in an entirely different context by the team, but if you're doing it right, people are going to realize that what you're asking them to do is important—not just a set of irrational demands—and they're going to do their best to achieve whatever goal is set before them.

Using a football analogy, it's very easy to throw a sixty-yard pass only to find yourself getting a holding penalty and having to go back and start over. Although it eats away at your time to only gain three to five yards on run plays or short passes during a game, you can continue to drive down the field. By having a leader who continually applies very deliberate pressure based on conditions, who presents a steadfast posture that shows his decisions are not rash but are well thought out and based on strategy and rules, the team will continue to work toward the end goal.

Taking care of your team is about looking at the whole as a collective and applying pressure accordingly—as you deem necessary. You must be balanced and upfront about your demands; don't ask one individual to do something that the team altogether could not achieve. You must uphold and apply the same standards to everyone.

But, at the same time, you must recognize that some individuals have more experience or talents that others do not possess, which will be discussed in patience. Positive pressure that is managed appropriately can inspire and develop people while ensuring standards. This shows the team that you're standing up for the organizational values, purpose, and goals.

Taking care of the team is also about making sure that you are appropriately rewarding your people when their actions lead to the achievement of certain goals or objectives. This includes rewarding individuals for going above and beyond normal expectations, even when they ultimately don't succeed. Often, people equate rewards to monetary value. In fact, Google has a program where it actually rewards people monetarily for good ideas, even if those good ideas fail. But we've seen that the current generation also responds to incentives that are about more than just dollars and cents. Workers today are looking for a healthy balance of professional and social contribution and involvement inside and outside of an organization.

As a leader, you need to be creative in finding ways to incentivize team members to be able to do the best they can, and that can be done in any number of ways. For example, there are a lot of ways you can get creative with work schedules, telecommuting, and virtual workspaces that allow people to contribute from anywhere. It's a huge incentive for people to be able to contribute to a team, but it becomes counterproductive if it is forced participation.

By rewarding effort through incentives, you're maintaining positive pressure on people to do the right thing. At the same time, adherence to ethical decision making and organizational standards and discipline must remain at the forefront.

Remain Steady and Balanced

Leaders get focused on what they need to do on a day-by-day basis; critical and creative thinking can become nonexistent and very short term, and dialogue stops, other than higher headquarters directing mundane tasks to be done. Despite the norm, you must overcome these detractors, or "squirrels," by taking a risk on what is more important to the welfare of your people and your organization.

A steady approach in time management and self-control will build a spirit of comradeship, enthusiasm, and devotion. People will begin to thrive, but as time goes on some teams or people's ability will wane. You must remain cognizant that different teams or subordinate leaders will have different endurance levels—some may flounder quickly and others will just get on with the job.

Leaders need to understand when and how to increase or decrease pressure on individuals or teams. Great leadership recognizes strengths and weaknesses. This situational understanding within your organization allows leaders to manage appropriate pressure over time, which permits people to thrive and stretch themselves in rising to meet any challenge. This awareness is your responsibility as the leader.

Most organizations desire stability and growth, and leaders want high-performing people and quality production all the time. But achieving this takes many years. This is where strong, quality leadership, a focused recruitment and retention strategy, and adaptable and agile processes enable great pressure management. But you need to manage pressure by adhering to values, purpose, and goals. By doing this, you can maintain influence and keep a landscape view of what is going on from an emotional and psychological perspective.

Do Not Fear Failure

Sometimes in today's fast-paced, rabbit-chasing environment, because things change quickly, leaders try creative ways to solve or prevent certain problems. Unfortunately, many leaders are working with people who are anchored in the ways of the past and are unwilling to change. As a result, when certain goals are not met, leaders tend to want to punish people for not achieving goals. Or they begin to fear their own failure, and as a result they begin to rule by decree. They begin to create more of an "I" situation, where they're just calling all the shots, versus a "we" situation, where the team has input. This in itself is their failure because they're not adapting to this new multi-generational workforce that is facing many challenges.

To promote an environment that experiences more wins than failures, you must ensure you're providing your team with the time, energy, space, and resources to do the work they've been tasked with. Without these provisions, you're setting the team up for failure— and ultimately you, as the leader, are responsible for that failure. You can't make anyone achieve a goal or work at their best by simply demanding that they do so; you must give them what they need to get the job done. Again, you must manage the pressure!

As the leader, you cannot fear failure of your team, nor should you always resort to punishing your team for failing. No one ever has a 100 percent success rate throughout his career. And if you fear that your team is going to fail or you punish them for failing at a task, you're going to create an environment where people are just going to quit trying to be innovative or use initiative. Again, leaders own failure, and the teams own success. Simply put, when you're involved, you must understand the pressure on the organization and take the appropriate steps to ensure success.

The way to maintain that positive pressure is by approaching problems with your team through "what if?" scenarios: "What if this happens?" "Does it matter if it does happen?" This can help improve your odds of developing a team that does not fear failure, because the team is prepared to react to change and manage inherent risk. We have discussed this before—serve people, listen to them and adjust if necessary, and give to them.

As the leader, you must constantly balance the desire to succeed (and not fail) with encouraging members of the team to try and not fear failing. This balance can be achieved by having options on the table, some of which may not work but for which you will still reward the team for its effort. By allowing for failure to occur without punishment, and subsequently rewarding effort, you're actually placing positive pressure on the team to succeed.

Dan Morgan:
The Importance of Relationships

Recently I attended an Army leadership school. We spent twelve days discussing leadership approaches based on past lessons from corporations and from within our own military. We also learned about where our Army plans to go in the future, looking out to 2025. This vision helped me understand where I needed to take my next command of an organization and our people to meet this vision.

I also spent two days receiving feedback from senior mentors based on a 360-degree assessment. Here is what I learned about myself:

- My superiors had great comments. Although I believe they are genuine in their remarks, I also believe in large part that those remarks were driven by successful results by the organization I was in command of at the time.

- My subordinates seemingly felt the same way.

- My peers, however, rated me lower on the scale than my superiors and subordinates. This was interesting and concerning.

The common theme in my peer comments was my aggressiveness and the pressure I put on my leaders and organization. I drove them hard, and it created a perception that maybe I was more important than the organization. I know that this is not true. I had a mission and put pressure on us to achieve it. I learned that I might have been able to do it differently, based on my peers' comments. Comments indicated that they were proud of their accomplishments and mission success—a combat deployment to Afghanistan. However, they felt I may not have been aware of the pressure.

I did not manage the pressure well. I pushed the team along the strain phase too long and was not aware as much as I should have been. It was a successful command and leadership and with a great climate. But I could have made it better.

In addition, this lack of self-awareness in my leadership and my organizational pressure was tied to my passion, another weakness of mine. I maintained a good sense of posture but I also needed to improve in pressure management by being quicker to listen and slower to speak.

As you rise as a leader with more responsibility, you move into a smaller world where relationships are more important. Leaders operate more independently—"it's lonely at the top," so to speak. And when you come together as a senior leader team, you do not want to jeopardize your relationships.

David Morgan:
Leading by Example

A number of years ago we had been awarded a contract to develop a new technical approach to provide an advanced surveillance solution with the Army. It was intended to fuse numerous sensors and cameras that had never worked together before. The concept was to create a unique way to provide remote surveillance capability to identify, locate, and track people moving around in contested areas. It had yet to be done as a complete, integrated solution, and there was plenty of risk and challenge involved in navigating the unknowns of systems that were never designed or intended to work with one another.

We ramped up our team and charged into the challenge; none of us had done anything like it before.

Like many projects, at first it was exciting, and we made a lot of progress quickly. But then the difficulties set in. After all, the systems were never intended to be used the way we were using them: radars designed to detect moving vehicles and tanks used to identify people crawling in the grass.

We spent boundless effort trying to figure out how to make the systems talk to one another and then give us data that actually made sense. The only way to do that was to run extended tests outdoors in a real environment.

Finally, we progressed to a point where we had a demonstrable solution.

The systems test was going to be held in the middle of Texas in the height and heat of summer. To validate the systems performance, members of the team had to walk long distances for long periods of time. Since we had limited staff on-site, and most of them were technical staff to troubleshoot the products, we ended up having to rotate the responsibility to be the target. I made sure that everyone there pulled duty taking that long, hot walk, and that started with me. I took the first shift and then made sure that I pulled more than my fair share, walking in the hottest part of the day or when the rains came and turned the dirt to mud. I was the senior executive on the ground and an owner of the company, so I could have used that time to conduct other business. But as a leader, you must not ask someone to do something that you would not do yourself. So that was my opportunity to literally walk the walk.

Leading by example means that no one was above being part of the team. We all had a role to play, and by showing that our company value statement was more than just words on a PowerPoint chart, we set the expectation that no one person is more important than the success of the team. Not only did we set the message and the standard, it gave me the opportunity to experience what every other member of the team experienced. Instead of sitting in an air-conditioned operations center trying to understand what the field was telling me over a radio, I understood it personally because I was in their shoes. I have done this on every program since. You cannot lead if you do not know who and what you are leading.

CHAPTER 10

Patience

"She generally gave herself very good advice (though she very seldom followed it), and sometimes she scolded herself so severely as to bring tears into her eyes; and once she remembered trying to box her own ears for having cheated herself in a game of croquet she was playing against herself ..."

J ust like in Alice's adventure, chasing white rabbits can be exhausting.

As a leader, being patient is having the ability to withstand the physical and psychological discomfort that comes with not getting your way or not getting what is expected. This habit is very difficult for leaders who are expressive, drivers, or extroverts. However, this does not mean that introverts or passive leaders do not get impatient or angry. Sometimes, any leader of any type needs to get stuff done, based on "squirrels," directives from superiors, and a lack of time or resources. It just happens.

Again, posture, pressure, and patience are mutually reinforcing. You must maintain a posture that conveys your values and those of your organization, and by managing organizational pressure you will begin to build an organization that works together. But you cannot manage pressure without being involved and soliciting feedback—and then doing something with the feedback. This constant cycle builds the requisite trust for the necessary innovation, inspiration, and inclusion that leads to success. But to pull all of this together, leaders need the final P: patience.

So how do we build patience in leaders to help their organization? It is not a short-term effort.

Take Care of Yourself

Taking care of the team begins with taking care of yourself.

Posture and positive pressure help you enable your organization to start doing the right things, innovatively, inspirationally, and, obviously, through inclusion (because everybody is a part of the solution). But to do those things as a leader, it begins with making sure you have the things you need to function properly.

And only you can figure out what those needs are because everyone is different. Are you a spiritual person? Are you physically in good health, in good shape? Do you eat the right foods to build strength and mental alertness? Are you getting enough sleep to help you recover physically and mentally?

A good portion of leadership is introspective, thinking through ways to become a better leader in promoting the vision. Leadership is also focused on trying to develop and become a better person and role model.

It can be difficult to be reflective and to develop oneself while also trying to manage teams of people. But without a team, a leader is just a party of one; you're not really leading anything if you're isolated. Leaders must take time to reflect and look deep, not only for themselves but for the well-being of the organization and people.

The patience component is about people. And in addition to developing people you work directly with, you must also develop those that provide an indirect support function to you as a leader. If you don't have others in your life helping to balance you out socially or to share responsibilities at home, if you're not allowing yourself to decompress and enjoy life through friends and social interactions, you don't have the collective whole together.

For that to happen, however, you must realize that not everybody's going to see the world the way that you do. They're not going to have the same pressures; they're not going to have the same intensity to take on all the same challenges and then try to achieve certain goals.

Leaders must realize that there are times where you have to try to literally unlock yourself from the position that you see yourself in and take the time to decompress and allow the team around you to congeal and support you. That takes a tremendous amount of self-control and patience.

Once you do this, you'll start to realize how you can impact the change that you need to in order to help the team produce more and to be able to achieve the goals that you've set out.

Patience in Decision Making

Patience as a leader is about realizing that you can't make dramatic changes overnight; you have to make incremental steps continuously and repetitively to be able to achieve your goals.

Perhaps the most difficult area in which you must practice patience is when you're making decisions and leading and developing your team to assume more responsibility and achieve more goals. As you're watching the team develop, you also have to encourage the members of your team to make themselves better by letting them make decisions. But that's part of leadership: leading key people in an uncomfortable situation where there aren't a lot of defined variables that will allow you to predict the outcomes. So sometimes it is best to let your people wade through the challenge and solve the problem.

In reality, some decisions can be delayed for a time—although not making a decision is, in itself, a decision. Still, sometimes leaders must be willing to sleep on a problem overnight; this allows you to absorb and consume the information presented to you. As mentioned earlier, in the military, sleep is viewed as a weapon because if you don't sleep, you are not investing in the intellectual energy and the emotional energy that you need in order to make the appropriate decision, particularly when you're in a combat environment. You need patience to display a posture of rigid self-control.

By allowing people to push themselves into uncomfortable situations where they're going to develop professionally and personally, you'll experience a double impact: Their ability to understand risk in decision making will instill more confidence in them, which will then make them more comfortable in taking on new challenges that encourage them to make greater strides toward their own goals.

When you allow people to make decisions within an organization, you develop them as someone who makes decisions and understands the risk piece of the process. The key here is to realize that their decision may not turn out the way anyone expected, in which case you'll be alongside them watching their options or course of action falter.

If that happens, your reaction will be key. You must have the patience to remain calm, to help them understand why what they're doing is not turning out the way it was supposed to and to motivate them to try again. In truth, the failure may have been caused by factors beyond anyone's control.

When making decisions, you must also have the patience to recognize which options are better than others. For example, once you begin to execute a mission in the military, everyone has a vote: The enemy has a vote. Weather has a vote. Time has a vote and so on. Understand this, and you can be patient. This acceptance enables you to recognize potential decision points that could indicate a change in direction is needed to reduce risk and increase odds for success. You must be agile and adaptive and prepared to shift from a known point to another direction in order to succeed.

Multigenerational Leadership Challenges

A leader's patience is truly tested when working in today's multigenerational workplaces; wrangling this white rabbit is a real challenge for leaders.

Why? Because a disconnect exists between today's generations, resulting in an increased level of difficulty for leaders to communicate with everyone in the workplace. This disconnect has been caused by anchor biases from each generation. And it is time for leadership—a responsibility for others—to align multigenerational organizations in order to develop inspiration, innovation, and inclusion.

While multigenerational differences are real, they tend to be less dramatic and contentious than the articles and studies suggest to readers. For example, leaders cannot overlook that millenials and baby boomers both desire financial security and opportunity. With such similarities, leaders must determine these shared concerns and facilitate interactions among the young and old.

Leaders, regardless of their generation, should look for innovative ways to bridge the generation gap. Organizational leaders need reciprocal relationships, regardless of age, gender, and race, where people share expertise and knowledge. Everyone sees the world in a different way, and that point of view must be valued. This is the challenge, "the white rabbit," for a leader—understand how people of different ages view the world and then develop strategies that leverage multigenerational strengths and encourage people to achieve organizational values, purpose, and goals.

Older generations in the workplace feel threatened by flatter organizations that are more common in today's workplace. The baby boomer generation believes that they should come to work and do their job, that their job is something that is in the best interest of the company, and that their efforts are mapped forward. And they believe if they work hard, they'll get promoted. It is a simple process that is reinforced by hierarchical authority.

Younger generations, on the other hand, take advantage of the access to information that's available to them, and they want to know why they're doing what they're doing and then how they're able to contribute to the organization. These generations, Generation X and millenials, are hitting their sweet spot and finding their roles as leaders. More and more, the younger generations look at a job as a way of life and that their contributions are more than just putting in a hard day's work. They would like to have the flexibility to work in different ways or locations. Outside of the service industry, people can access information and work from just about anywhere, at any time. This flexibility can be as big a driver as money, and there are many examples where people take greater flexibility over pay.

At the end of the day, the outcome that these generations want is the same. They want to feel valued. They want to feel appreciated. They want to be compensated for what they are doing.

Where the two generations diverge is in the knowledge/experience argument.

In today's environment of the Internet at your fingertips, information is a commodity—there's an overwhelming amount of information available through immediate and free access. You can find an answer to anything on the Internet; the question is whether it's correct or relevant to your job or what you're trying to achieve.

The problem is that younger generations instantaneously get information and generally believe that information to be knowledge, whereas older generations believe knowledge is gained with experience. This is a constant debate in the workplace; just because the information is out there doesn't mean it is fact. The older generation tends to view information as research material, data with intellectual and institutional value that they can absorb and understand and then roll into their experiences.

So the understanding of what information is versus what experience is varies widely. It's essentially two extremes, and crossing between those extremes is always a challenge. Therefore, part of your responsibility as the leader is to be able to work between the generations. It's up to you to explain to the younger generation how information doesn't automatically translate into knowledge and that knowledge based on experience far outweighs just having information.

As the leader, you must also have the patience to work through the experience gap between the different demographics on your team and to understand that they're not going to have the same point of reference on everything that you're explaining to them. It takes patience to communicate in ways in which your team members are going to be able to accept the information, apply it to their framework of how they see the world, and then understand how they can use that information to contribute to the team. You're not going to be able to say the exact same thing to people from different demographics and assume it's going to be communicated.

At the same time that you're trying to communicate across the generations, you must be self-aware and humble enough to recognize that you may not understand generations other than your own, and you may not fully grasp the latest life concerns, technologies, or the skills that affect different generations' perspectives. Still, it's up to you to gain as much understanding as you can, use the tools at your disposal, and unite the generations in your organization.

Leaders must foster a diverse, inclusive culture that listens and adjusts to differing views across the organization—including seasoned veterans and young entry-level employees. Leaders should consider structured leader development, varying compensation packages, healthcare, and incentives that are flexible and meet the needs of the multigenerational organization—it is worth the effort.

Leader and Team Development

The reason it's crucial to have patience and use various methods when communicating across multigenerations is to develop leaders for the future.

To stress a few points again: When you're trying to train, develop, and manage a team to achieve a higher level of performance, getting your point across is key to success. Without having the patience to communicate your message so that everyone understands it, you'll kill development because people tend to shut down when they get frustrated. Sometimes, you just need the patience to stand back and allow things to develop, and understand when you need to insert yourself into the situation to give the team guidance and when you need to ensure they have the resources they need to develop on their own.

In addition to developing as professionals, you may also need to ensure your people have what they need to develop in their personal lives. Why? If they don't have the ability to deal with the stresses in their lives, you're not going to get the most out of them. And it takes a tremendous amount of time and energy and patience as a leader to observe whether your team members are developing correctly.

When it comes to developing other leaders for your organization, sometimes that means sending them to get training or education. Although you run the risk of the individual taking that knowledge elsewhere afterward, in most cases that knowledge will come back to your organization and be beneficial for your company and for the individual. The long-term benefit of offering leadership development is that people will be drawn to your organization because you're known as a leader that invests in people and believes that people are the solution, not just information and technology.

There are times when it's just not going to be possible to accomplish a goal, or you can't understand why others take longer than you to accomplish the same goal. The bottom line is that just because you said a goal should happen doesn't make it so. Winning a championship doesn't happen by a leader walking in on day one and everyone congealing at 100 percent to win. You can't just say, "We're now great," and then everyone suddenly starts performing with greatness. Becoming an effective leader is a constant, continual, everyday process to incrementally get better—sometimes it takes years to realize that you've matured into a next-level leader.

Often, leaders think they can read a book or go to school or watch a seminar and suddenly become a leader, but none of these give you the foundation to lead an effective team where everyone immediately respects you as their leader. Leadership is a skill you've got to hone continually. And sometimes you'll accomplish goals rather quickly, and sometimes it takes so long to make a change that you'll forget you're even trying to get it done.

Leading takes time and a lot of repetitive practice. There will always be another rabbit to chase, another trial or tribulation that you cannot predict. You can't control when those opportunities arise where you must prove yourself as a leader in front of your team. In fact, it often seems like those opportunities get subjected upon you when you are on the verge of losing control—those are the times that really make or break you as a leader. So it's crucial to have the patience to realize that a lot of other distractions are probably going to be in place when that one chaotic moment arises when you most need to stand up and deliver.

People have different aspirations for being a leader. Some people don't ever aspire to be a leader but are thrust into that role. Other people spend their entire lives trying to be a leader for that one moment in time when their efforts will be recognized—a moment that may never come in their career. We've seen phenomenal leaders throughout history whose methods we study; these are leaders who have been in the right time and place to make a widely noticeable impact. But there are countless leaders that do great jobs every single day that don't ever get a real chance to publicly shine.

But leadership isn't about accolades. Leadership is about leading.

There are great leaders that do great things because they are being supported by the people around them. But at the end of the day, if you're really committing yourself to being an effective leader, then leadership is a solitary choice.

Dan Morgan:
Admitting You're Wrong

As a battalion commander, our base in Afghanistan was constantly receiving enemy rockets. We knew where the enemy was firing from, but the process to fire back on the target through preapproved air munitions was too time consuming, and it would not allow us to successfully counterfire against the enemy.

So I gave our staff some planning guidance and asked them to develop a plan. Our field artillery officer began diligently working on a plan with our operations chief, and then every week I asked him, "Where are we on the plan?" But over time, I lost sight of the plan because of other developing priorities. I failed to maintain the appropriate positive pressure, and my patience was running thin.

One day, the officer came back to me and started briefing me on the plan. He had performed analysis on the enemy and the terrain, identified key enemy targets for approval, and then had sent the information up the chain of command for approval.

What I wanted was the preapproved authority to fire based on conditions. But I took issue with him sending the plan up the chain of command for approval without first consulting me. In truth, it didn't need to be approved by me, and the officer was exercising initiative like I had pushed them to do. I just had not approved the conditions or the targets. He felt like he was empowered, and he came up with very innovative ways of resolving the issue. He was inspired by having a very complex problem to solve, and he had built an inclusive team to develop this concept of operation.

But when he came and briefed me, I lost self-control and yelled at him. I normally talk very assertively and directly, which this officer knew because he had been with me for over a year. However, this outburst was atypical. We had built an organizational environment of trust and transparency, collaboration, and collective responsibility within our organization and outside of it. I broke those values at this moment because I failed at patience as a leader.

Not only did I lose my patience during that particular moment, I failed the posture and pressure test as well—I wasn't consistent in my actions, and I violated our own standards and discipline.

All of these were tied back to the fact that I was not taking care of myself, and as a result I was tired, stressed out, and frustrated with other things that had nothing to do with this officer.

But it was too late: He was visibly shaken by my reaction, and he walked out because I told him to.

A few hours later, I came to my senses and realized that I had made a horrible mistake. I sought him out, and, exercising complete transparency, in front of everyone that was in his vicinity (maybe another fifteen officers and staff), I placed my hands on his cheeks, looked him directly in the eyes, and apologized to him.

Then I backed off and in a voice that everyone else could hear, I explained what had happened and apologized to him again in front of my whole staff.

I had failed at the "Three Ps," but as soon as I recognized my error, I admitted my mistake. I needed to immediately rebuild relations and realign with my staff based on our values, purpose, and goals. If I did not, I could lose much more than I had gained over the past years with these soldiers. Again, I had a learning moment about leading others through responsibility.

David Morgan:
The Best Worst Decision

As you progress through life, the very first time you meet a challenge or begin a new adventure, time seems to speed up and everything is more intense. After time, things tend to slow down a bit and you start to pick up the finer details. However, in the fire service there is still intensity on almost every call, as you have no idea what you are truly going to find when you get there or when you open the next door. There is always a bit of an edge or nervousness. We used to say that if you did not get nervous anymore, it was time to hang it up. You had lost the edge of being able to be aware. Decisions like that cannot become a simple transaction. There is too much at stake.

Typical scenes are chaotic to say the least. There are fire trucks, police, victims/patients, bystanders, and even media on the largest of incidents. Incoming vehicles have sirens blaring, and people—crews and civilians—are typically asking you questions, while all the time you have someone on the radio barking in your ear about updates. Trying to make sense of it all while you are still trying to focus on your job is difficult at best.

One of the biggest challenges in leadership is trying to keep your teams focused in times of stress and be diligent when things are going well.

I remember one night early into my time as the chief, we responded to a horrific crash in one particular area that was notorious for high-speed accidents. As I arrived on the scene, there were multiple cars with a number of victims in each. As we triaged the scene, we realized that there was one victim in one car and a family in the other. Both cars were mangled and a mess of twisted metal and broken glass. The ground was slippery with oil and fluids that were leaking from the cracked engines.

The one man's car was overturned on its side after rolling several times. He was just lying there, halfway out of the car, unconscious with a vacant stare. The family's car had been hit broadside with all the windows blown out. They were barely moving, and all the doors were jammed shut due to the twisting after impact.

As we went to work on the cars, I found out we were dramatically understaffed on the apparatus on the scene, and we had no more help coming. After a quick evaluation, the man in the car did not appear to have a pulse or breathing. Struggling with decision to prioritize, I quickly assessed the patients and directed all of the resources to extract the family.

As I stood there on the scene, with the smell of the diesel engines and the scene lit up by the lights on the fire trucks, every once in a while I kept glancing back at the man in the car. At times I thought I could see him move. It's not like in the movies—his eyes were still open and when I looked at him, it was like he was looking at me. Did he have a pulse? Was he still alive? Did I just decide that this man was to die? Those thoughts kept racing back in my mind and still do today.

Throughout the incident the crews stayed focused on exactly what I asked them to do. Get the family out. They were dedicated to the task at hand and worked as a team.

After we got the family out of the car and off to the hospital, we redirected our efforts to the man in the car. Although his upper body was relatively unscathed, his legs were a tangled mess. At that point it was reconfirmed that he had passed away.

Later, the crews got back to the station and we did an after-action review, which was a standard practice on all calls of significance. They questioned the approach. Did we do the right thing? Could we have saved him? What if …? The reality was that there was no way to ever know. If we had chosen to remove him, he would have most likely died regardless. And who knows what would have happened to the family had we prioritized differently. But we had made a decision, and that decision was the best one at the time with the conditions and information we had.

It was incidents like this that galvanize a team. We understood that in the face of adversity you had to make decisions, and sometimes it is the best of the worst choices.

———————————————————————————

PART FOUR

Who Do You See in the Mirror?

"Who in the world am I? Ah, that's the great puzzle."

Just as Alice pondered the change in her world—and in herself—we, too, have learned much about ourselves since we began our journeys.

There is a huge challenge for leaders today to have the time to reflect on what they've accomplished. Are you who you think you are? Are you what you think you are? And from the overall perspective of a leader and as an individual, have you achieved what you've aspired to achieve? These are very difficult questions to answer with all the competing interests in your world and in your life potentially consuming your time and getting in the way of your thought processes. It is a hard thing to be able to take the time to reflect and appreciate all that you have and all that you've become.

While we've combined our thoughts on leadership up to this point, the next two chapters are our individual reflections on where we are today.

CHAPTER 11

Who Does Dan Morgan See in the Mirror?

"If you don't know where you are going any road can take you there"

Today, I will tell you I'm a leader, but I'm also a human being, which means that, like other human beings, I'm flawed. I may choose the wrong path or make the wrong decision. The question is, have I done the best I could, and will I do the best that I can do today? Did I see a piece of trash on the ground and pick it up? That's really what it boils down to.

I am a lifelong learner of leadership. I want to be part of something bigger than myself. I hope to be part of positive change and preferably significant change. I also want to love those around me who help me and allow me to help them. This is my purpose, and I have chosen serving men and women in uniform as the conduit for fulfilling my purpose. This is my journey, and I will take any road I believe right.

I have seen many versions of Dan Morgan in the mirror over the last few decades. I have seen a young man who challenged authority—sometimes at the expense of losing everything. I have also seen an insecure young leader who never quite knew if he was meant for his profession or doing his job well enough. I still see that on occasions today. I have seen a tough, hardened man from five combat deployments as a ranger infantryman. But I have also seen that same man broken and crying from stress, resulting from being around soldiers killed in combat, suicides, and a stressed but still going strong marriage.

But I chose to be a leader. I chose to be responsible. I chose to want to be part of something bigger than me. That is my profession as a military officer. And it is my personal profession as a husband and father.

As a leader committed to values and people, you will reach a point in life where you will have undergone a physical transformation and will begin to wonder, "How do I get back to what I used to be?" But you can't. Your experiences will have changed you. Your body will undergo change. You'll grow older. You'll be responsible for other people: maybe a spouse and children, maybe even your parents. And when you are older, you will not be able to do the things you did when you were young. You cannot drink beer like you used to. Running hurts. You cannot bench press the same amount of weight. It sucks. But if you are giving to others, you are earning wisdom.

As we grow and mature into our leadership roles, we wake up in the morning and see ourselves in the mirror and think, "Who in the world am I?" That's the great puzzle. This is what the discovery of leadership over the last couple of decades has been about for me. That is what it means to chase the white rabbit.

As a leader, you're not perfect. But what do you see every morning in the mirror, based on the organization that you have chosen to be a part of? How are you making sure that you're becoming better, not only for yourself but for everyone around you?

When I look in the mirror, I see someone who is still growing and learning. And because I'm flawed, I still make mistakes. But that's okay because when I look in the mirror, I ask myself, "Can I live with the mistakes I've made?" If I can, that means I'm learning from them. And I must continue to be transparent enough to impart those mistakes and lessons learned on other people so they can understand and learn from them.

So when I look at myself in the mirror, I ask myself, "Who am I today? What am I going to be tomorrow? Can I continue to provide the positive energy for myself and for others to accomplish something that's bigger than myself?" If I answer yes to those questions every morning, then I know that I'm on the right path of making positive change, and I'm still chasing the white rabbit.

CHAPTER 12

Who Does David Morgan See in the Mirror?

When I look in the mirror, I see a person who, through some happenstance and a lot of hard work, had the opportunity to get on the field to compete; I competed in a lot of different games and became comfortable and confident in my own ability to do what I do well. From that, I feel confident that with any opportunity that I embrace going forward I will be able to commit 110 percent of who I am as a person to be able to achieve that goal. I know that I will not succeed in everything that I do, but what I am confident of is that at the end of each day, I will have committed to put in everything that I possibly could. There will be no feeling that I could have done more.

Along the way, I've been very fortunate to meet some incredible leaders in the fire department, in the military, and in industry.

And what I've learned is that your perception of who truly is a leader versus whose name is on the organization can be two very different things. I've found that some of the most charismatic, motivated, intellectually stimulating people are not the people that we identify in most cultures today as leaders. Yet some of the guys who are the most humble, hardest-working people, who don't get the notoriety, have impacted me the most as leaders; those are the ones that resonate with me.

One thing that has really settled in with me is the importance of truly understanding yourself and what you believe in. It is those individuals who get wrapped up in the cloak and notoriety of a title who can so quickly get dragged down into poor decisions. There are very few opportunities in life where a single individual is a game changer and critical to success. There is always a network of supporters, peers, and coworkers that are with you through every decision or crisis. Regardless of how impactful you can be, you need the rest of your team, stakeholders, customers, and community to come to any progress.

Everyone has their own individual reasons that drive them to get up and compete every morning. Whether or not it is personal, professional, financial, or otherwise, one belief does not outweigh another. What matters is the belief in your own values and how you relate these to what you are trying to accomplish. This must be ever-present in all that you do and align with your team's mission and goals.

I have experienced the reality that no matter how critical you may think you are today, tomorrow you are replaceable. Change happens, and people continue to move on. If you are becoming a leader for accolades, awards, or some other recognition, you may have a long wait. At the end of the day, you have to do it for yourself and your team. No one may understand the sacrifice and commitment it took, and you have to be comfortable with that.

It's been a pretty challenging path to get where I am today. There have been more than enough dark days—struggling to just get enough food on the table and being the constant underdog that was always being counted out. And through it all, I've gained a much greater appreciation of what leadership truly is and how much of it is a personal commitment to be the best person you can be to motivate and deliver the environment for your team to succeed.

CHAPTER 13

Conclusion

L et's face it, leading is ultimately a solo venture. It can be a very lonely experience because, in the end, everyone in the room has a leader—except the leader. You are the only person in the room who has to make a decision—and others are counting on you to make that decision.

True leaders tend to live and breathe their roles. Being a leader is a lifestyle choice, and sometimes—because leaders normally deal with multiple problems or move constantly and quickly from one problem to another—it's very difficult to turn off the role. In essence, it can be a real challenge to compartmentalize when you're dealing with problems every hour, every minute of the day.

Although leadership responsibilities don't end when the workday is through, that doesn't mean that you must be always on, that you must always be the decision maker or the person you are in the office.

Leadership becomes who you are, not what you are. It doesn't mean that you have to have a title such as "CEO"; that doesn't define a leader, as we've seen all too often in recent years. Leadership is about your perspective in life, about owning your choices, and about the core values that you maintain every day, all day.

Leadership is a choice of lifelong learning in the pursuit of meaning for people and their organization. It is the symbiotic relationship of your values with one of an organization and its purpose and goals.

Leaders face ethical, moral, and legal challenges that create dilemmas in decision making. These choices, along with other risk management, truly define your journey—the chasing of the white rabbit. Find these challenges and make the best decision with your team and for the organization. And be responsible for it.

We hope that this book has given you the opportunity to take the time to reflect on yourself and ask: "Have I achieved what I'm trying to achieve? Who am I as an individual? Who am I as a professional? As a spouse or parent? And how can I make myself better?"

When you look in the mirror, have you put everything that you could into your decisions so that regardless of what comes tomorrow—right or wrong, if the company loses money, people lose their jobs, or someone loses a life—will you still own the risk of the decision that you made? We hope the values in this book give you that ability to continue to improve your decision making and your ability to challenge yourself as a leader.

To be a leader, you must continually put yourself in an environment that requires you to lead. A person can be a CEO and not be a leader, but you can also be a leader and not be a CEO—you can be an average person leading the baseball league, you can be a leader at home just raising kids, you can be a leader just being a student.

As a leader, often there is no defined path for you to follow. Understand that you'll never be a perfect leader. You're going to make mistakes. There are significant unknowns out there that are going to affect your ability to lead, and you're going to have to challenge yourself every day to understand that and know that you don't have full control—and never will have full control of every situation. But if trust exists within your organization and among its people, you will affect positive change and success.

As a leader, you're going to have to decide for yourself that this is who you want to be because it becomes a way of life. It doesn't matter who you lead: If you're happy doing what you're doing, then keep doing it. Whatever it is that you love to do, just keep getting better at it. You must continuously put yourself in situations, whether physically or through mental exercises, where you ask yourself "what if?" so that you can be better prepared to make decisions based on things that might actually occur that require your leadership.

The journey can never end. You're going to continue to learn. You're going to continue to experience. You're going to continue to chase white rabbits. You're going to continue to evolve as a person professionally and personally. That's going to allow you to make better decisions and hopefully be able to be a better leader to your team, your family, and anybody's life that you can influence.

You're always going to have to challenge yourself every day to get better, and you must never discount the gift of feedback. That's what makes you a leader.

ABOUT THE AUTHORS

Dan Morgan

Dan Morgan is an active duty infantry colonel in the US Army who graduated from Georgetown University in Washington, D.C., where he earned a bachelor of arts degree in international affairs in 1992 and a master of arts degree in national security strategic studies in 1998. Currently, Colonel Morgan serves as the Joint Base Commander of Joint Base Lewis McChord in the State of Washington, where he delivers installation support and services to enable the readiness of joint Army and Air Force operational forces.

He has served in Vicenza, Italy, as part of the 3-325th Airborne Battalion Combat Team (ABCT), which is NATO's spearhead rapid reaction force for Europe and Africa. After returning from Italy, Colonel Morgan was afforded an opportunity to serve as a GS 13/14 Executive Assistant to the Presidential Cabinet Officer, Director, White House Office of National Drug Control Policy. During this period of 1998–2001, he participated in Executive Office of the President, interagency, and legislative policymaking activities. His duties included extensive domestic and foreign travel in support of the United States National Drug Control Strategy. Under President Bill Clinton's administration, he engaged at the highest levels of service in the government of the United States and with foreign governments ranging from Colombia to China.

Upon completion of his White House service, Colonel Morgan returned to active duty and was assigned to the 101st Airborne Division (Air Assault) in 2001 through 2011. During this assignment, he served as an Air Assault Company Commander, Battalion Operations Officer, Brigade Operations Officer, and Division Chief of Operations, where he participated in over four years of combat—two deployments to Iraq and two to Afghanistan.

From 2011 to 2014, Colonel Morgan was stationed at the 10th Mountain Division (Light) where he commanded the 1st Battalion, 87th Infantry Regiment. In January 2013, he deployed the battalion to Regional Command-East in Afghanistan for his fifth combat deployment. Following this deployment and command privilege, Colonel Morgan was assigned as the 10th Mountain Division Chief of Staff (Rear) from 2013 to 2014.

Colonel Morgan spends most of off time with his wife, Patty, and children, Isabel and Gabriel, who are competitive athletes in lacrosse and wrestling. In between deployments, work, and family, Colonel Morgan tries to spend time hunting and fishing where he can relax and regain the physical and mental energy needed to provide for others. His favorite books that shape his leadership and always near him are Doris Kearns Goodwin's *Team of Rivals: The Political Genius of President Lincoln*, Ulysses Grant's *Memoirs*, *Narrative of the Life of Frederick Douglass: An American Slave*, and Viktor Frankl's *Pursuit of Meaning*.

David Morgan

David Morgan is cofounder and chief operating officer of STS International, where he oversees worldwide operations responsible for rapid design, development, and deployment of cutting-edge anti-terrorism and physical security technologies, medical simulation training applications, and professional engineering services. Through his innovations and strategic leadership, STS has achieved significant growth by penetrating new and emerging markets through a diversified client base in eighteen countries across four continents.

David Morgan has led the development and deployment of programs to protect national interests for the Department of Defense, including the Department of the Army's biometrics program and the Department of the Army and the Navy's intelligence, surveillance, and reconnaissance (ISR) technologies. He has deployed technical subject matter expertise to meet urgent Warfighter program requirements in Iraq, Afghanistan, and other austere locations. And he has led the development of medical simulation technologies for the Army, Air Force, Navy, and Marines.

His strong commitment to research and development has translated his strategic vision into reality by producing technological and logistical advancements in the way in which US forces are supported in mission critical operations. Advancements include: advance body armor solutions that were recognized in the Army Greatest Inventions program; command and control technology that consolidates full motion video (FMV) into common display systems; forming unique, highly skilled teams to provide sustainment operations, logistical support, and training to US forces throughout Iraq, Afghanistan, and other locations around the world for ISR and counter-improvised explosive device (C-IED) systems for the US forces deployed; secure information screening, analysis, transfer, and dissemination in support of intelligence operations; and establishing the foundation and original program architectures for the development and integration of biometric technologies into DoD operations.

David Morgan's core leadership principles are grounded in the strong belief that the investment in talented staff—and challenging the very best in his staff—is the greatest investment a company can make. Under his leadership, STS has grown almost 300 percent in the last three years. Most recently, STS was recognized as one of Inc.'s 5,000 Fastest Growing Companies in 2014 and 2015 and was a 2014 Small and Emerging Contractors Advisory Forum (SECAF) Government Project of the Year award finalist.

As a small business entrepreneur, Morgan has a true passion for mentoring young and emerging entrepreneurs. He served as board of director member to a nonprofit and is currently on an advisory board of several private companies. He is a regular speaker on innovation and entrepreneurship at the University of Maryland Smith School of Business and Georgetown University Law School. He is a member of the Dingman Center Angels, who evaluate and invest in premier start-up technology companies. Recognized for his leadership and evaluation of emerging technologies, David Morgan has been named to the National Institute of Justice Peer Review Panel and is an active reviewer of innovative approaches to analysis, research, and development; information and sensor technologies; investigative and forensic science and technology; and law enforcement technologies. He is a contributor to McGraw-Hill Publishers as a technical editor, reviewing training materials and publications for first responders and homeland security professionals in emergency operations and disaster response.

Based on his experiences, he has served as an advisor to many emerging professionals and over ten small businesses that span the defense and commercial industry. His community leadership and philanthropic efforts focus on service and include serving the community as a member of the Laurel Volunteer Rescue Squad and Prince George's County Fire Department for over two decades and supporting our nation's military through activities such as the Fisher House organization and Wounded Warrior programs.

Printed in the USA
CPSIA information can be obtained
at www.ICGtesting.com
JSHW012051140824
68134JS00035B/3381